THE GREAT
ROCK 'N' ROLL
QUOTE BOOK

THE GREAT
ROCK 'N' ROLL
QUOTE BOOK

EDITED BY

MERRIT MALLOY

ST. MARTIN'S GRIFFIN   NEW YORK

Design by Sara Stemen

LIBRARY OF CONGRESS CATALOGING-IN-PUBLICATION DATA

The great rock & roll quote book / edited by Merrit Malloy.
    p.   cm.
    ISBN 0-312-13504-1
    1. Rock music—Quotations, maxims, etc. 2. Rock musicians
—Quotations.   I. Malloy, Merrit.
ML3534.G74   1995
781.66—dc20

95-30179
CIP
MN

First St. Martin's Griffin Edition:

10 9 8 7 6 5 4 3 2 1

CONTENTS

INTRODUCTION

Rock and roll began for a few and is now a part of all of us. It has become part of our lives to the extent that a certain melody, a song, a personality can easily hurl us back to another time another place, it becomes a spirit that moves us. The rock-and-roll culture has and is now playing its part in influencing our lives.

The composers and performers of rock and roll have created words, sounds, terms, and catch phrases that surround us today. They have in a way become our heritage.

The selections in this book have been chosen from a vast possibility of choices. They will make you laugh, cry, think, and surmise, but most importantly they will take you back to a time be it fifteen minutes or twenty years ago. Rock and roll lives on.

—Anonymous Rock 'n' Roll star
(wishing not to fall prey to commercialization by self-promotion)

ADVICE

Be strong, believe in freedom and in God, love yourself, understand your sexuality, have a sense of humor, masturbate, don't judge people by their religion, color, or sexual habits, love life and your family.   **Madonna**

Find out who you are and what you stand for, and learn the difference between right and wrong; be able to weigh things.   **Prince**

Just rock on, and have you a good time.   **Duane Allman**

You can't base your life on other people's expectations.

Stevie Wonder

Instead of always looking at the past, I put myself ahead twenty years and try to look at what I need to do now in order to get there then.

Diana Ross

In the spirit of Dr. King and our national holiday of peace, I'll smile like the fox and cheer like the cheerleader, raging Americans to exhibit the character that will heal us as a nation.   **Stevie Wonder**

ALTERNATIVE

I think heavy metal fans are more open-minded than people give them credit for.   **Bruce Dickinson**, Iron Maiden

[On his duet on "Do Wah Diddy Diddy" with the alternative band Mary's Danish]: I think they're great. Of course, my mother thinks I'm playing with someone's breakfast.   **Neil Diamond**

[Singer/poet on the genesis of the legendary X album *Los Angeles*]: The thing I found incredible about Los Angeles was the flagrant inequality. You'd be on the Sunset Strip with people dangerously close to attacking you for money while all these Rolls-Royces were going by.   **Exene Cervenka**

Christ was a punk rocker.   **Billy Idol**

We just observe from the outside and comment, like an alternative news service.   **Mark Chadwick**, The Levellers

It's pretty easy to draw parallels between the war being waged now against rap and the kind of resistance that greeted the early rock and rollers of the

Fifties. To paraphrase Pete Townshend, it's not for us to judge the music that's being made in the streets; we just have to get out of the way.

Vernon Reid, Living Colour

With the punk thing, everyone was making impractical attacks on being rich or having money, ya know, but they all wanted to be rich.

Boy George

You can't just sit there and wait for people to give you that golden dream. You've got to get out there and make it happen for yourself.

Diana Ross

When I was a Beatle, I thought we were the best fucking group in the world, and believing that is what made us what we were. **John Lennon**

We want to be phalluses ramming in the butthole of pop.

Gibby Haines, Butthole Surfers

I don't know how—I just did it. It was just that time when anybody could form a band.   **Poly Styrene**, X-ray Specs

I'd rather have ten years of super-hypermost than live to be seventy by sitting in some goddamn chair watching TV.   **Janis Joplin**

There is nothing about my career that is an accident.

Marc Bolan, T-Rex

When he was three, he said he'd be a star.

Mettie Baker, Prince's mother

I knew, I had no qualms, nothing. I was going to sing, and I was going to sing rock 'n' roll.   **Ronnie Spector**

Achievement is for the senators and scholars. At one time I had ambitions, but I had them removed by a doctor in Buffalo.   **Tom Waits**

When I left Tucson, I thought it would be a big deal to have your name on the marquee of a club. That was the pinnacle of success. I never dreamed I'd have a number one record.   **Linda Ronstadt**

APPEARANCE IS EVERYTHING

I remember calling up *Variety* and accusing the Beatles of stealing my look. The woman there said, "Look, sir, let me tell you something. Their hair is like the Three Stooges, not yours!" **Tiny Tim**

[ZZ Top guitarist on why he and bassist Dusty Hill refused a hefty sum to shave off their trademark beards for a Gillette commercial]: Can't do it, simply because underneath 'em is too ugly. **Bill Gibbons**

The biggest misconception people have about me is that I'm stupid.

Billy Idol

Sometimes, you like to let the hair do the talking! **James Brown**

A rock 'n' roll band needs to be able to get under people's skin. You should be able to clear the room at the drop of a hat.

Paul Westerberg, formerly of The Replacements

Madame Toussaud's will have my statue. I just hope they don't make me look like James Brown. **Little Richard**

They look like boys whom any self-respecting mum would lock in the bathroom! But The Rolling Stones—five tough young London-based music makers with doorstop mouths, pallid cheeks, and unkempt hair—are not worried what mums think!

> Anonymous journalist in the *London Daily Mail* sometime in 1963/64

[About Patti Smith]: All I could think about her was B.O.—she wouldn't be bad-looking if she would wash up and glue herself together a little bit.

> **Andy Warhol**

The worst thing that ever happened to me was when platforms went out of style.

> **John Oates**, Hall & Oates

He [Frank Zappa] had every social disease. I think that's possible. . . . He was infested, and so was his hair. He hadn't taken a bath for months. Or combed his hair. I think it was not so much rock 'n' roll, and not so much the road, as it is [sic] that nobody was taking care of him. You can always spot a bachelor!

> **Gail Zappa**

ARROGANCE

I would think nothing of tipping over a table with a whole long spread on it just because there was turkey roll on the table and I had explicitly said, "No turkey roll."
Steven Tyler, Aerosmith

I could be unbelievably horrible and stupid. On tours, I'd get on a plane, then get off it, maybe six or eight times. I'd walk out of a hotel suite because I didn't like the color of the bedspread. I remember looking out of my room at the Inn on the Park one day and saying, "It's too windy. Can someone please do something about it?"
Elton John

When you're as rich as I am, you don't have to be political.
Sting

I had alienated all the nice people I knew by being the general, predictable slave to the myth of rock 'n' roll stardom.
Michael Des Barres

What people say means absolutely nothing. When the record comes out, it's like a receipt for me to say "fuck off."
Bill Laswell, Material, The Golden Palominos

AUDIENCES

The life of a rock 'n' roll band will last as long as you look down into the audience and can see yourself, and your audience looks up at you and can see themselves. **Bruce Springsteen**

. . . Historically, musicians have felt real hurt if the audience expressed displeasure with their performance. They apologized and tried to make the people love them. We didn't do that. We told the audience to get fucked.

Frank Zappa

Our main audience is about eighteen years old. People that age don't really understand music that much. . . . If they were really that musically hip, they wouldn't even like us. **Ritchie Blackmore**, Deep Purple

I think that at U2 concerts it seems to me that the audience almost applaud themselves. . . . When they hear songs from a few years ago, their own memories are woven into them. **Bono**

Never did I think I'd become family entertainment. **Jimmy Buffett**

Many a night I would be out onstage, and the intimacy of the songs against the raucousness of this huge beast that is an audience felt very weird. I was not David to that Goliath.   **Joni Mitchell**

Like when you wake up that morning and as soon as you're awake enough to remember, "Oh, I'm goin' to a concert tonight," you call up your best friend. You get excited, you figure out what you're wearing, you decide where you're gonna meet, and then you meet, and you go to the venue, and you see all these other people, and you get more excited. Then the opening act comes on, and you're more excited. And the lights go down and, whoa!

Joan Jett

I wish I would tell our audience that we don't hate them without sounding cheesy.   **Kurt Cobain**

Thinking about why society turned on us [The Rolling Stones], I think they must've sensed our arrogance, our "You're so boring, and we're so great," that kind of thing. They knew that. People always do. . . . It makes the public determined to show people like us where God lives.

Marianne Faithfull

BABY BOOMERS

We lit candles and sat around listening to John Lennon sing with genuine passion in his voice about how he was the egg man, and they were the egg man, and he was also the walrus, and, by God, we knew exactly what he meant.
Dave Barry, humorist

I look at Nirvana and Soul Asylum and I practically get acid flashbacks.
Jann Wenner, *Rolling Stone* publisher

Getting old is a fascinating thing. The older you get, the older you want to get.
Keith Richards

I've led a pretty clean life, so I've aged pretty well.
Bobby Sherman

We're fucking forty-year-old men, and we're behaving like children. It's silly, absolutely fucking idiotic. Retarded.
Eric Burdon, The Animals

People have this obsession: They want you to be like you were in 1969. They want you to, because otherwise their youth goes with you, you know?
Mick Jagger

[On his band's sold-out Los Angeles concert]: I think I exploded the myth that rock 'n' roll is just for young people.

Paul McCartney, at age forty-seven

We grew up dancing the Twist, the Mashed Potato, the Boogaloo, the Jerk, the Watusi, the Pony, the Alligator, the Clam, and the Vicious Bloodsucking Insect. We knew the dirty words to "Louie Louie," including the ones that did not actually exist.   **Dave Barry**

I'd rather be dead than singing "Satisfaction" when I'm forty-five.

Mick Jagger

BAND NAMES

You can call me Jimmy or you can call me Iggy. My parents called me James Osterberg, Jr. Iggy was a nickname hung on me that I didn't particularly like.

Iggy Pop

I was playing in an all-night jam session, and I had cut my finger and I didn't know it. When they turned the lights on at the end, the organ keyboard was covered with blood. So I called everybody over and said, "Wouldn't this make

a great album cover for a band called Blood, Sweat and Tears?" And so we called it that, except we didn't use that picture because no one had a camera.
Al Kooper, founder of Blood, Sweat and Tears

[Singer/songwriter/guitarist on how her band came to be named The Pretenders]: I was hanging out with this guy who was in a motorcycle club. One day while visiting their "clubhouse," he took me into his room and bolted the door shut. He wanted to play me his favorite record, but he didn't want any of his "brothers" to hear it. . . . It was Sam Cooke singing "The Great Pretender." I looked at this white supremacist lowlife, with his hand on his heart and his eyes shut, swaying to that clear, black voice, and I thought, "I'll have some of that."
Chrissie Hynde

I wake up some nights and think, Orchestral Manoeuvres in the Dark? What a stupid name! Why did we pick that one?
Andy McCluskey

We'd never heard of the movie. It just sounded like a funny name. Then I found out about the film and saw it. I hated it.
Kevin Shields, My Bloody Valentine

Taxi drivers, our mothers, feminists, men—no one likes it. It was obscene to everybody.
Viv Albertine, on the name of her band, The Slits

This big rat just happened to scuttle along at the very moment I was telling them I had scabies.
Rat Scabies, The Damned

... We, Barry Melton and myself, finally signed a piece of paper which he interprets as saying that he is "The Fish." So when we play together in a week or so, it'll be "Country Joe" McDonald and Barry "The Fish" Melton. It's evolved to that. He's become a lawyer, so we don't argue with him anymore.

Country Joe McDonald

We didn't even know we were The Beach Boys until the song came out.

Mike Love

We didn't realize that with eleven letters in Brownsville, most of our marquee appearances at rock/hippie theaters would have our name reduced to "Brown Sta."

Cub Koda, guitarist, on his days in Brownsville Station

Yeah, they thought we were a low-rider band—they thought we were "Die Cruisin." **Dan Kubinski**, Die Kreuzen

The band's name means the act of dying, but, like, really mega!

Dave Mustaine, Megadeth

I once told this writer a story about how I met the guys in an elevator and found out that we all had the same last name, so we decided to form a band.

Joey Ramone, The Ramones

... I didn't know what doobie meant. ... Dyno [Rosen, a friend who suggested the name The Doobie Brothers] had been reading *Rolling Stone* and pointed out this paragraph: "... as they were smoking a doobie." I said, "Rosen, what does this mean?" And he said, "You idiot! It's a joint."

John Hartman

We had fuck-all to do with Asia, but it's a good word.

John Wetton, Asia, King Crimson

The Beatles is probably one of the worst names anyone ever came up with, but as soon as you get used to it, it represents the best band in the world.

John Wetton

The Modern Lovers' name came to be the day after Jonathan Richman decided to form a band. Jonathan wanted a name to describe the kind of love songs he was going to make. He figured they would be modern ones.

Jonathan Richman, speaking in the third-person on the name of his band

If you look at all these band names, they're just really stupid names; and the more stupid the name, the more outstanding it is, I guess. Or the more memorable.

Keith Morris, The Circle Jerks

I wanted a name that would put us first in the phone directory, or second if you count ABBA....

Martin Fry, ABC

We were called The Toilets originally—we were flushed with success.

Mike Peters, The Alarm

McAFEE

[On how the former Declan Patrick McManus became Elvis Costello (Costello is his mother's maiden name.)]: I hadn't picked the name at all. Jake [Riviera, his manager] just picked it. It was just a marketing scheme. "How are we going to separate you from Johnny This and Johnny That?" He said, "We'll call you Elvis." I thought he was completely out of his mind.

Elvis Costello

I mean, you say, "aha" all the time. Our manager says that this band has been on everybody's lips for years.   **Morten Harket**, Aha

[On the naming of Buddy Holly's backup band, The Crickets]: ... We did consider the name "Beetles," but Jerry [Allison] said, "Aw, that's just a bug you'd want to step on," so we immediately dropped that.

Niki Sullivan

[On the umlauts over the O and U in Mötley Crüe]: We didn't think about its [umlauts] proper use. We just wanted something to be weird, and the umlaut is very visual. It's German and strong, and that Nazi Germany mentality—"the future belongs to us"—intrigued me.   **Nikki Sixx**

We were throwing around names when off the top of my head I blurted out, "Temptations".... Bill [Mitchell] said he really liked it. But when he asked the other four their opinions, we all took one look at ourselves in our raggedy, long winter coats and cracked up. We knew we weren't likely to tempt anyone or anything, but what the hell, it was as good a name as any.

Otis Williams

[The Ramones lead singer on the selection of his band's name]: It had a ring to it, like "Eli Wallach" does. Just sounded good.   **Joey Ramone**

[On naming the band Butthole Surfers]: Oh, no, no regrets at all. My mom even says it now. It took her about ten years, but I've heard her say it two or three times now.   **Paul Leary**

I had friends who had a band called Wild Kingdom. Then Mutual of Omaha said, "You can't use Wild Kingdom." So they changed their name to The Gospel Birds. Then a couple of months later someone gets a hold of them and says, "You can't use Gospel Birds because there's a gospel group called The Gospel Birds." So then they became The Zulus, and nothing's happened. They've been all right—except their record label dropped them.   **Reeves Gabriels**

... Two of the guys [members of The Soft Boys] were half-Jewish, so we could have sort of called ourselves The Psychedelic Jews but it's the sort of thing that offends Jews and goyim alike. You're just going to piss everyone off. That's part of the appeal, really. Like calling an album *Queer for Jesus*, y'know. It's very tempting, if you want to deal with the torrent of misunderstanding that follows.   **Robyn Hitchcock**

I came up with the name, The Del Lords.... There were The Del Bombers and The Del Diamonds, and I always thought that was the coolest thing in the world.... One night, me and a friend of mine were sitting around watching TV, smoking a bunch of pot, eating Häagen-Dazs, and watching the Three Stooges. I always say it was like in *West Side Story* when Tony sees Maria, how the whole room goes dark and there's a spotlight. This episode was produced, written, and directed by Del Lord.... It's like, what does God have to do, actually come down and deliver the pizza himself, y'know?

          Scott ''Top Ten'' Kempner

[Denying that his band's name was inspired by Sinclair Lewis's classic *Arrowsmith*]: No way. That was just some book that they made you read in high school.   **Steven Tyler**, Aerosmith

[Tongue-in-cheek explanation for the name of the all-female punk/heavy-metal band, L7]: We say it's Lesbian Seven. We say it's a level of consciousness when you get to level seven in meditation. We say it's lubrication, a love jelly called L7. There's actually a guitar amp called L7.... There's also a panty size L7—large seven—very apropos for this band.

Suzi Gardner

[On trying to conceal that the name, The Doobie Brothers, refers to marijuana]: Uh, it's a French family name. We went so far, seriously, as to go to a radio station that was square and straight and go, "Doobie? Haven't you heard of Romper Room?"   **John Hartman**

[On The Circle Jerks' name]: We had some feminists say that, "Well, it's kind of a male kind of thing." And we said, "I guess women could do it, too, if you used your imagination."   **Keith Morris**

[The Butthole Surfers' guitarist on some earlier band names]: We started out as The Dave Clark Five back in San Antonio, Texas. We had this deal about wanting to change the name of the band for every show we did, so the next show we were The Dick Gas Five, and then we were Nine Foot Worm Makes Own Food. Then we started playing in Austin as that. And then we were The Vodka Family Winstons and we were Abe Lincoln's Bush. Then we were The Inalienable Right to Eat Fred Astaire's Asshole, and then the next show we were just plain The Right to Eat Fred Astaire's Asshole.   **Paul Leary**

BEGINNINGS

One month Artie [Garfunkel] and I were watching "American Bandstand" on television, and the next month we were on the show. It was an incredible thing to have happen to you in your adolescence. I had picked up the guitar because I wanted to be like Elvis Presley, and there I was!   **Paul Simon**

I think it was in 1967 that John Lennon said, "The dream is over." And, in 1977, I remember thinking the same thing. But it doesn't have to be over. There are those of us that are still dreaming, still trying to breathe life into the old forms of rock 'n' roll. Rock 'n' roll has given so much to me, and I want to give something back, but I don't want to be part of what it's become, this ugly monster, this dinosaur. There's this story of Saint George stabbing the dragon with his sword. Well, we need a few Saint Georges around here.   **Bono**

Naturally they [early rockers] sound as if they could care less, so long as their little black 45s hit number one and made them rich and famous. But they delivered a new version of America with their music, and more people than anyone can count are still trying to figure out how to live in it.

Greil Marcus, journalist and author of *Mystery Train:
Images of America in Rock 'n' Roll Music*

[On the early days of The Rolling Stones]: With Mick's thin voice and the musicians we had, I never dreamed we'd catch on. Never, never, never.

Ian Stewart

[The Rolling Stones long-time session keyboardist on his early days playing with the band]: But to tell the truth, I sure as hell wasn't impressed with these guys. It was obvious that Brian [Jones] was a flake from the things he said. Mick and Keith looked like a couple of Picadilly panhandlers. . . . Every day they wore the same stuff, which they probably slept in. . . . When these guys all got together in the closed confines of that rehearsal room, believe me, it was a pretty gamy place.   **Ian Stewart**

. . . He'd [Gram Parsons] come out of the house with Keith [Richards], skipping along . . . in these faggy outfits, and the other guys would say, "We can't go onstage with this fucker."

Jim Seiter, backup musician for Gram Parsons

[On the pre-rock days]: It seemed to me that Negroes were the only ones that had any freshness left in their music.

Sam Phillips, producer, Sun Records

There was this place called the Almus Pharmacy that was next door to a hearing-aid store, and on Tuesday nights they'd open up the hearing-aid store and roll away the racks of these hearing aids. They'd have these kung fu shows. They called 'em like The Ridiculoids, and there were these two bands called The Againsters. . . . The Againsters were against everything, and The Againsters were doing shit over and over. Cleopatra's Vagina was a killer band. Jesus, that was a long time ago. **Paul Leary**

When we moved to England . . . we had nowhere to live, nowhere to go, no food—we were buying a hamburger at McDonald's and splitting it three ways and sharing the last french fry. **Slim Jim Phantom**, The Stray Cats

[On his days touring with Buddy Holly]: When they called 'em rock 'n' roll pioneers, they were talking about the music. But that pretty much described the living conditions, too. **Waylon Jennings**

THE BUSINESS

The whole music business in the United States is based on numbers, based on unit sales, and not based on quality. It's not based on beauty, it's based on hype and it's based on cocaine. It's based on giving presents of large packages of dollars to play records on the air. **Frank Zappa**

We've made our deals with the devil. **Huey Lewis**

Probably the biggest bringdown in my life was being in a pop group and finding out just how much it was like everything it was supposed to be against.
Mama Cass Elliot, The Mamas and the Papas

What pisses me off is when I've got seven or eight record company fat pig men sitting there telling me what to wear. **Sinéad O'Connor**

There always was some kind of payola, but it was much smaller than what I hear goes on today. You know, twenty dinners in a week, a hooker for the night, maybe even a color TV, but that was it.
Ellie Greenwich, songwriter

A recording studio isn't much different from a factory. It's just a factory for music. **Van Morrison**

All we had ever heard about record company people was that they were vampires and criminals and they killed Elvis Presley.
Björk, formerly of The Sugarcubes

The whole business is built on ego, vanity, self-satisfaction, and it's total crap to pretend it's not. **George Michael**

You get to the point where you have to change everything—change your looks, change your money, change your sex, change your women—because of the business. **Mick Jagger**

You're a local band until you get a record contract, then all of a sudden Bruce Springsteen is your competition. **Sammy Llana**, The BoDeans

Not even boot camp is as tough as being in rock 'n' roll. **Patti Smith**

I've been in slavery all my life. Ain't nothing changes for me but the address.
James Brown

CREATIVITY

Creation is like trying to get through a wall. You can blow it down and get to the other side quickly, or you can take your time and build a door. I guess stuff [drugs] will get you there faster, but which one do you think will leave you with a roof still over your head? **Eddie Van Halen**

[When asked which of his compositions were the best]: The ones where I just held the pen. **Kris Kristofferson**

I have to create. I have to dig in the earth; I have to make something grow; I have to bake something; I have to write something; I have to sing something;

I have to put something out. It's not a need to prove anything. It's just my way of life.   **Bette Midler**

I do my best work when I'm in pain and turmoil.   **Sting**

I wasn't forced into this business, I did it because I enjoyed it and because it was to me as drawing breath and exhaling it. I did it because I was compelled to do it, not by my parents or family, but my own inner life in the world of music.   **Michael Jackson**

The guy who wrote "Handy Man" [Jimmy Jones] tried to sue us over "Karma Chameleon." I might have heard it once, but it certainly wasn't something I sat down and said, "Yeah, I want to copy this." We gave him ten pence and an apple.   **Boy George**

Artists everywhere steal mercilessly all the time and I think this is healthy.
                                                              Peter Gabriel

CRITICS

[About rock 'n' roll]: It is sung, played, and written for the most part by cretinous goons; and by means of its almost imbecilic reiterations and sly, lewd—in plain fact, dirty lyrics—it manages to be the martial music of every sideburned delinquent on the face of the earth. This rancid-smelling aphrodisiac I deplore.   **Frank Sinatra**, 1957

The Beatles are not merely awful; they are so unbelievably horrible, so appallingly unmusical, so dogmatically insensitive to the magic of the art, that they qualify as crowned heads of anti-music.   **William F. Buckley, Jr.**

Writing about music is like dancing about architecture—it's a really stupid thing to want to do.   **Elvis Costello**

In the Top Forty, half the songs are secret messages to the teen world to drop out, turn on, and groove with the chemicals and light shows at discothèques.
                                               Art Linkletter

I will sit down with anybody that has criticized my work negatively; I will sit down with them and make them eat shit.
                          August Darnell, Kid Creole and the Coconuts

Fighting the American press is like disobeying your parents, because they're so pompous a lot of the time. In live concert reviews they treat you like opera! "Mr. Costello did this" . . . and so forth. **Elvis Costello**

The kids today are quite right about the music their parents listened to: most of it was trash. The parents are quite right about what their young listen to: most of it is trash, too.

Gene Lees, "Rock," *High Fidelity*, November 1967

[Little] Richard's records all sounded as if they were made in the Saturday night uproar of a turpentine logging camp. His raw, strident voice was torn from his throat in a bawling, shouting torrent that battered and scattered the words until they sounded like raving.

Albert Goldman, *New American Review*, April, 1968

Remember when you used to watch TV in the Sixties and you'd see Perry Como in a cashmere sweater? That's what rock 'n' roll is becoming. It's your parents' music. **Neil Young**

The Beatles are a passing phase. They are the symptoms of the uncertainties of the times. **Billy Graham**

All of the rock music being aired today is demonically inspired. Any individual listening to it is entering into communion with a wickedness and evil spawned in hell.

Jimmy Swaggart, evangelist and cousin of early rocker Jerry Lee Lewis

[On MTV]: I'd rather that you waited all week with some feeling of anticipation for one program that was genuinely great, in which you saw good bands that were exciting, than have twenty-four hour access to a load of idiots with too much money and not enough sense.   **Elvis Costello**

[On the need for cleaning up rock]: I'm a fairly with-it person, but this stuff is curling my hair.   **Tipper Gore**

With these vulgar fractions of the treble clef, I wish you luck with a capital F.   **Elvis Costello**

CYNICISM

You now have a nation of kids who don't read. The bulk of information that enters their brains comes from television or records . . . so control over those sources of information is rather attractive to an authoritarian mentality.

Frank Zappa

I made a mistake thinking that rock 'n' roll had something to do with being intelligent and not accepting society as it was being given to us.

Anonymous

We want to be the band to dance to when the bomb drops.

Simon LeBon, Duran Duran

Most people are so hard to please that if they met God, they'd probably say yes, she's great, but ... **Diana Ross**

All rock 'n' roll is plagiarism. I think more people should admit it and do it better. **Anonymous**

I've got a phone, answering machine, TV set, computer, hand grenade—everything you need to run a business in Los Angeles. **Ice-T**

I like to think of us as Clearasil on the face of the nation. Jim Morrison would have said that if he was smart, but he's dead. **Lou Reed**

Anybody that walks can sing. **Michael Stipe**

I never met Johnny Rotten, but I like what he did to people.

Neil Young

DAZED & CONFUSED

You're talking to someone who really understands rock music.

Tipper Gore

Women are great. When they dig you, there's nothing they won't do. That kind of loyalty is hard to find—unless you've got a good job.

David Lee Roth

I'm very driven, even though I don't drive.　　**Debbie Gibson**

The more I see, the less I know for sure.　　**John Lennon**

Rock 'n' roll really changed my life. I heard Little Richard and Jerry Lee Lewis and that was it.　　**Elton John**

Everybody I've seen, like Little Richard, Jerry Lee Lewis, and all those sort of people, I'm afraid, are extremely pathetic.　　**Elton John**

Everybody asks me if I sing on this record. Even my mother asks me. Fabrice and I—I think we are big talents. We can sing as well as any other pop star in the Top Ten.　　**Rob Pilatus**, Milli Vanilli

I was doing folk rock when there was no such thing as folk rock.

Roger McGuinn, The Byrds

The only time I ever punched Tina with my fist was the last fight we had. I hit her after she kneed me in the chest. Prior to that, our fights, or our little slaps, or whatever they were, were all just about attitude. . . . It was always because she was looking sad and wouldn't tell me what was wrong with her on the stage, and that would really depress me. So after the show, I'd end up slapping her or something. But then we'd be okay.   **Ike Turner**

My favorite show is "People's Court," 'cause I love to see people lie.

Vince Neil, Mötley Crüe

I'm always trying to figure out why people don't appreciate Duran Duran.

John Taylor

I like Beethoven, especially the poems.   **Ringo Starr**

I don't listen to music. I hate all music.   **Johnny Rotten** (John Lydon)

My first drug experience was sniffing glue. We tried it, and moved on to Carbona. That's why we wrote songs about it. It was a good high, but it gave you a bad high. I guess it destroys your brain cells, though.

Johnny Ramone

It's a nice place Michael [Jackson] comes from. I wish we could all spend time in his world.   **Steven Spielberg**

I don't even know
my own phone
number.

Axl Rose

SHAI

There's three of us in the band, so we split everything straight down the middle. **Mitch Mitchell**, The Jimi Hendrix Experience

I'm pro-heterosexual. I can't get enough of women. I have sex as often as possible. . . . It's really hard to maintain a one-on-one relationship if the other person is not going to allow me to be with other people. **Axl Rose**

DEFINITIONS

Rock 'n' roll is like an aphrodisiac for people who have everyday jobs.
Slash

Rock journalism is people who can't write interviewing people who can't talk for people who can't read. **Frank Zappa**

Work is life, you know, and without it, there's nothing but fear and insecurity.
John Lennon

Rock 'n' roll meant fucking, originally—which I don't think is a bad idea. Let's bring it back again. **Waylon Jennings**

Negotiation means getting the best of your opponent. **Marvin Gaye**

Madonna is closer to organized prostitution than anything else.

Morrissey

We're labelling it "soul bubblegum." **Berry Gordy**, on The Jackson 5

Five guys on stage sounding like World War III.

Les Paul, on heavy metal

I once asked him [John Lennon], "What do you think of what I do? What do you think of glam-rock?" He said, "Aww, now. It's great, you know, but it's just rock 'n' roll with lipstick on." **David Bowie**

I don't know what grunge is. That's like buildup on your windows.

Jerry Cantrell, Alice in Chains

Soul is the way black folks sing when they leave themselves alone.

Ray Charles

A musicologist is a man who can read music, but cannot hear it.

Sir Thomas Beecham

THE DOWNSLIDE

You wonder about people who made a fortune, and you always think they drank it up or stuck it up their nose. That's not usually what brings on the decline. It's usually the battle to keep your creative child alive while keeping your business shark alive. You have to develop cunning and shrewdness, and other things which are not well-suited to the arts.   **Joni Mitchell**

Out on the streets, I couldn't tell the Vietnam veterans from the rock 'n' roll veterans. The Sixties had made so many casualties. Its war and its music had run power off the same circuit for so long, they didn't even have to fuse. The war primed you for lame years, while rock 'n' roll turned more lurid and dangerous than bullfighting. Rock stars started falling like second lieutenants. . . .   **Michael Herr**, author of the Vietnam War memoir *Dispatches*

Nobody loves me but my mother, and she could be jivin', too.

B.B. King

White folks play Vegas, don't they? It's the thing you do when you don't have no hits, when you don't have no choice.   **Jackie Jackson**

I'm shopping around for something to do that no one will like.

Jerry Garcia

That's what happens to some pop superstars. They wind up in a corner, singing to themselves.   **Marshall Chess**, cofounder, Chess Records

DRINKING & DRUGS

When I was a practicing alcoholic, I was unbelievable. One side effect was immense suspicion: I'd come off tour like Inspector Clouseau on acid. "Where'd this cornflake come from? It wasn't here before."

Ozzy Osbourne

My credo: When I get scared and worried, I tell myself, "Janis, just have a good time." So I juice up real good, and that's just what I have.

Janis Joplin

You know, where taking drugs used to be a gas, it just got to the point where it wasn't fun anymore. It was the only thing that made any of us outrageous and crazy. Tommy [Lee] and I couldn't go a day without a drink. It gets to be a very private pain.   **Nikki Sixx**, Mötley Crüe

On one occasion we were in a clinic in Switzerland, Keith [Richards] in a room on the ground floor, me up on the third floor. We used to call back and forth to each other from our balconies, bragging about whose new blood was better.   **Andrew Oldham**

I definitely have a responsibility to talk negatively about heroin. It's a really evil drug. I think opiates are directly linked to Satan.   **Kurt Cobain**

Somebody has to let them [youth] know that it's not hip anymore to do drugs; that there will be pressures and times in your life when you'll need answers, but that coke and the rest offer nothing—no outlet, no information. And believe me, you're only as good as your information.   **Bob Seger**

[On his band's downward spiral into drug addiction]: I guess we just had more fun than humans are allowed to have.   **Tommy Lee**, Mötley Crüe

Everybody gets fucked up, man. Everybody gets fucked up sooner or later. You're just pretending if you don't let your music get just as liquid as you are when you're high.   **Neil Young**

The most deadly thing about cocaine is that it separates you from your soul.
                                                 Quincy Jones

I was basically on about a triple acid trip right when they asked me to play at Woodstock. Which answers the question: "Can a man play his own songs when he couldn't find his car?"   **John Sebastian**

[An acid-tripping Jones on the Rock of Gibraltar reacting to the sudden dispersal of a simian group when he turned on a tape of music he had recorded for a film]: The monkeys don't like my music! Fuck the monkeys! Fuck the monkeys! **Brian Jones**, as recounted by Marianne Faithfull

The only way we made it was with a great big old bag of Mexican reds and two gallons of Robitussin HC. Five reds and a slug of HC and you can sleep through anything. **Butch Trucks**, drummer, The Allman Brothers Band

I don't drink because I'm an alcoholic. I drink because I love to party. **Bret Michaels**, Poison

[About hangovers]: It's only pain. It'll go away. **Slash**

I was a successful junkie for about a year; the only reason I was able to stay healthy and didn't have to rob houses was because I had a lot of money. **Kurt Cobain**

I didn't really want to enjoy the moment. I wanted to take drugs. **Doug Fieger**, The Knack

I had it made in the heart of Cheever country; the big house on the Sound, a beautiful wife, two children, the luxury car, the whole shot. But no country club, just a one-thousand-dollar-a-day drug frenzy. **John Phillips**

We couldn't do the amount of drugs we wanted and be a band, so we ended up doing the drugs. **Paul McKenzie**, Enigmas

To summarize The Pretenders, all I can say is that we were the genuine article. In fact, we were so genuine, we killed ourselves. . . . We never had any pretensions. If it sounded dangerous, it was because it was dangerous.

Chrissie Hynde

Of course, every day that you stayed up longer—and there's things you have to do to stay up that long—the impending tiredness and fatigue produces that hallucinogenic state quite naturally. Well, half-naturally. By the end of the week, my whole life would be transformed into this bizarre, nihilistic fantasy world of oncoming doom, mythological characters, and imminent totalitarianism. Quite the worst.   **David Bowie**

Long-term peace—except maybe "rest in peace"—is not found in a chemical. Being half-conscious always slaps back.   **Grace Slick**

I wouldn't take a shot for a million dollars in cash money—and that's a damn lie.   **Jerry Lee Lewis**

[On why he doesn't do heroin, 1979]: . . . People who like smack also like Lou Reed, and that can't be anything in its favor.   **Lemmy**, Motörhead

[On the preferred drug of each of The Bee Gees]: I was the piss artist, Barry was the pothead, and Robin was the pillhead.   **Michael Gibb**

Drugs and sex go hand in hand when you're a rock 'n' roll musician. Whereas if I were a violinist, it might be a little different.   **Slash**

[At the Third Annual Great Atlanta Pot Festival]: The government doesn't want you to have a good time, and sometimes your parents don't want you to have a good time. Guess what, baby? The Black Crowes want you to have a motherfucking good time.   **Chris Robinson**

[On Jimmy Buffett's rescue of two seamen in the Caribbean, and the ensuing celebration]: He's amazing. He turns a shipwreck into a party.
Tom Corcoran, Jimmy Buffett band member

If we burn ourselves out with drugs or alcohol, we won't have long to go in this business.   **John Belushi**

I won't be happy until I'm as famous as God.   **Madonna**

What's so hard about being Mick Jagger? What's so tough? This exaggerated sense of who you are and what you should do and worrying about it so much.

Why don't you just get on with it and stop trying to figure out all the angles? That to me is a waste of time.   **Keith Richards**

I thought we stood for infinity.   **Mick Jagger**

When I do music, I include a lot of people, but nobody's really involved except myself. Just God and me. I guess I'm like Einstein—let 'em worry about my theory after I'm dead.   **James Brown**

I think I'm very entertaining, and I think I deserve all the money I get!   **Gary Glitter**

Nobody can do it as good as me.   **Joe Shithead**, D.O.A.

It's actually come as quite a shock to learn just how many people don't like me.   **Phil Collins**

I am the Nureyev of rock 'n' roll.   **Meat Loaf**

My ego is already inflated way past the exploding stage.   **Kurt Cobain**

I'm ambitious. But if I weren't as talented as I am ambitious, I would be a gross monstrosity.   **Madonna**

I've looked up to David Bowie all my life, but now I think he should look up to us.   **Ian McCulloch**, Echo and the Bunnymen

[On losing the cover story in *Time* magazine to Dwight Eisenhower's death]: Fourteen heart attacks, and he had to die in my week. In my week!

Janis Joplin

We had big ideas. I mean, as far as we were concerned, we were going to be the next Beatles or something. We were on a trip, definitely.

Jerry Garcia

I am bringing my genius to idiots who cannot go out and reach it for themselves because they are too stupid.   **The Great Kat**

Being spokesman for a generation is the worst job I ever had.

Billy Bragg

. . . It's always been my ambition to be killed by some lover in a fit of passionate jealousy.   **Marianne Faithfull**

The songs for the album *Timeless: The Classics* were selected on the basis of my ability to sing the hell out of them.   **Michael Bolton**

The song "Wanted Dead or Alive" is about the way we live. We are modern-day cowboys—we ride into town, put on a show, take the money, hit the bar, take the ladies, and we're gone.   **Richie Sambora**

There were guys I used to go to the clubs and watch, and I thought there must be a place in there for me, because I could sing as well as that geezer with the big lips in The Rolling Stones.   **Rod Stewart**

ELVIS

The hair was a Vaseline cathedral, the mouth a touchingly uncertain sneer of allure. One, two-wham! Like a berserk blender, the lusty young pelvis whirred and the notorious git-tar slammed forward with a jolt that symbolically deflowered a generation of teenagers and knocked chips off ninety million older shoulders. Then, out of the half-melted vanilla face, a wild black baritone came bawling in orgasmic lurches. Whu-huh-huh-huh f'the money! Two f'the show! Three t'git riddy naa GO CAAT GO!

Brad Darrach, *Life*, Winter, 1977

The opinions on Elvis grow petty with time. He was a man's man. A mama's boy. A native genius of the spirit. A tentative step above white trash. A vain hick. A valiant hero. The maker of some of the finest gospel and spiritual records ever released. A sacrilegious church truant. A loyal friend. A loutish bully. An archetypal southern gentleman. A low-living letch. A princely appreciator of his fans. A pasty-face pillhead. The rock voice without peer. The rock enigma without equal. The King ... One thing is certain: the sudden appearance of Elvis Presley on the scene was nothing less than the full-blown arrival of modern rock 'n' roll. By virtue of the white-hot urgency of that arrival, Elvis Presley became the "Mystery Train" he sang about in one of his early sessions, an unmarked locomotive rocketing down a jet-black track piloted by a specter, making an unscheduled stop. It was not the kind of train that brought things back.   **Timothy White**, *Rock Lives*

Where do you go from Elvis Presley—short of obscenity, which is against the law?   **John Crosby**, *New York Herald Tribune*, 1956

I consider it my patriotic duty to keep Elvis in the ninety percent tax bracket.
                    Colonel Tom Parker

Without Elvis, none of us could have made it.   **Buddy Holly**

He was singing and split his pants. One of his boys went to get him another pair, and threw the split pair in the corner. A girl who was working for the Methodist Publishing Company in the same building asked me what to do with the pants, and I told her, "You better hang onto them, that boy's gonna be famous." She said, "Naw." And there she was six months later on "I've Got a Secret" with Elvis's pants.   **Chet Atkins**

Mr. Presley made another television appearance last night on the Milton Berle show. He might possibly be classified as an entertainer. Or, perhaps quite as easily, as an assignment for a sociologist.
                    Jack Gould, *The New York Times*, June 7, 1956

I don't know anything about music. In my line, you don't have to.
                    Elvis Presley

Just remember
he did the
decorating—not
me!
**Priscilla
Presley**, on
Graceland

Elvis Presley

So Elvis Presley came, strumming a weird guitar and wagging his tail across the continent, ripping off fame and fortune as he scrunched his way. And, like a latter-day Johnny Appleseed, sowing seeds of a new rhythm and style in the white souls of the new white youth of America, whose inner hunger and need was no longer satisfied with the antiseptic white shows and whiter songs of Pat Boone.   **Eldridge Cleaver**, *Soul On Ice*, 1968

One small-town boy, born at the right time, in the right place, in the right environment, and under the right circumstances (represented by convergence) of all the musical currents in America's subculture: black and white gospel, country and western, and rhythm and blues.   **Anonymous**

FAME

It's been like a bad dream I never woke up from.   **Alex Chilton**

Even stars get tired of talking about themselves. Some of them can talk intelligently, but a lot of them can't even hold a decent conversation. They know nothing but rock, and not a lot about that. It makes it difficult to get a decent interview. A lot of times, you'll be lucky to get more than muttering and stuttering.   **Bill Graham**, concert promoter

That would just happen when I would introduce myself. "Hi, I'm Glenn Frey from The Eagles." And they would just look at me like, "Well, you must be the placekicker, because you're not big enough to play football."

Glenn Frey

Being a celebrity is not so great a gig, and it's not as good as being a good musician or having a particular skill. Celebrity always misses the point, and you end up disappointing the people who thought you were what you never said you were.

James Taylor

The worst part of having success is to try finding someone who is happy for you.

Bette Midler

Nobody deserves to have their personal life pried into like I did, and no one deserves to hear me whine about it so much.

Kurt Cobain

I got fame and fortune, and I lost my sense of reasoning.

Little Richard

I was always wondering if they really liked me or did they like my songs.

Neil Young

From being in the public eye, people perceive you differently. They all "yes" you to death when you need friends to tell you "no" sometimes. The hardest thing to find out is who your friends are. I think that in this position, people are looking at what you are and not who you are.

Tico, Bon Jovi

In Japan, they named a sake after me.

Suzi Quatro

Inside the clubs, it's all right; outside we get the shit kicked out of us.

Perry Farrell

Instead of Messiahs, we always had big rock 'n' roll stars. We like to see who we're worshipping.

Patti Smith

People used to throw rocks at me for my clothes. Now they wanna know where I buy them.

Cyndi Lauper

It [the backlash against The Rolling Stones] was really a reaction of society against what society itself had done. They had built us up too high, and now they would tear us down.

Marianne Faithfull

All the things I've read in my schoolbooks about England and the queen were okay, but my very eyes are the greatest book in the world. When we did the royal command performance, and then after it, I actually looked into the queen's eyes. It was the greatest thing!

Michael Jackson

The future's so bright, we gotta wear asbestos.

Pat Torpey, Mr. Big

FAMILIES

The definitive bomb-the-mom song has yet to be written, and would exorcise a lot of demons for a lot of people. **Billy Joel**

I'd never even picked up a baby before I had one. I just thought they were like a load of martians. **Chrissie Hynde**

My dad taught me about music. He used to tap dance. **Ray Davies**

A lot of Michael's success is due to timing and luck. It could just as easily have been me. **Jermaine Jackson**

[Remembering his father, John Lennon]: He was like a real dad, you know. We used to sit down with guitars and mess around.

Julian Lennon

You leave home to seek your fortune and, when you get it, you go home and share it with your family. **Anita Baker**

My son, just because of his presence, keeps telling me there is a sorrow, there is a future, and that there's no point in screwing up today; because every day that you screw up is going to have an effect, karma-wise, on the future.

David Bowie

We all come from dysfunctional families, and these days, I guess that's pretty normal. **Carnie Wilson**, Wilson Phillips

My father and I have the same hands. We have the same dreams. We write the same lyrics, sometimes. **Prince**

Rock and roll wives ... I hate 'em. Fortunately, there's only a couple of 'em around. But, honestly, I don't know how they have the nerve to continue in the face of their appalling failure. **Mick Jagger**

They say domesticity is the enemy of art, but I don't think it is. I had to make a decision: am I going to be just a family guy, or should I go up to London three nights a week, hit the nightclubs, occasionally drop my trousers, and swear a lot in public? I made my decision, and I feel okay with it. Ballads and babies—that's what happened to me. **Paul McCartney**

My parents love the new girlfriend and the new lifestyle. They even had me as a houseguest for a couple of weeks. They let me in the house. Gee, I think that's important. **Iggy Pop**

[On how his parents met]: Dad knocked Mom over as she was walking out of a store. He and his big brother Joe were running from the cops after pummelling four guys in retaliation for a whupping my father had gotten earlier. The police caught Joe, but Dad pitched Mom on her butt and kept on going. It was love at first sideswipe.   **John Cougar Mellencamp**

FANS

The typical rock fan isn't smart enough to know when he's being dumped on.   **Frank Zappa**

I happen to think if they're into me, they have a certain amount of intelligence.
                                                     Billy Joel

Just because you like my stuff doesn't mean I owe you anything.
                                                     Bob Dylan

My Daddy is my biggest fan. He's a minister, you know.   **Alice Cooper**

There are no more political statements. The only thing rock fans have in common is their music.

Bob Pittman, vice president, MTV

I wanted to get up and dance, but I wasn't allowed to in the royal box.

Princess Diana, after a Dire Straits concert

[On the fans the name of his band attracts]: ... All the halls are filled with these people in black gowns with candles, sitting on the floor chanting, and nobody from the hotel removed them. ... So we decided we'd open the doors all at the same time and blow the candles out, and sing "Happy Birthday" to them, see. Which we did. And, of course, they left.

Tony Iommi, Black Sabbath

I haven't been sent a turd. But some chap in Manchester who took exception to The Dammed wiped his bum and sent me the piece of paper through the mail, which wasn't too charming.

John Peel, BBC

[On The Grateful Dead]: We're constitutionally incapable of taking much seriously.

Bob Weir

Bible says that thou shalt not commit adultery. Moses got that law from God. It's a good law ... because back in those Bible days, if a man could have

six wives, three hundred concubines, and still commit adultery, I'd kill him myself.
Ray Charles

Once we three were at an exclusive party in the Hollywood Hills, invited there by Tom's [Waits] lawyer, and Rickie [Lee Jones] went right in, sat down, and put an avocado between her legs. Tom was embarrassed, but got a great kick out of it. Nobody would talk to us after that, so we spent the evening going up to people with cocktail dip hidden in our palms and shaking hands with them.
Chuck E. Weiss

If you want to torture me, you'd tie me down and force me to watch our first five videos.
Jon Bon Jovi

On my gravestone, I want it to say, "I told you I was sick."
Tom Waits

For most people, the fantasy is driving around in a big car, having all the chicks you want, and being able to pay for it. It always has been, still is and always will be. And anyone who says it isn't is talking bullshit.
Mick Jagger

I could never get along in a band with a posturing, posing lead singer.
Keith Richards, on Led Zeppelin

Q: What's the smartest thing you ever heard anybody in rock 'n' roll say?
A: Be-bop-a-lula, she's my baby.
Paul Simon

I guess I like to have fun.
Madonna

GIMMICKS

I like some of the showmanship and gimmicks of rock 'n' roll, whether it's Chuck Berry's duck walk, Pete Townshend's flailing, or the Sex Pistols's anti-promotion. I've heard TV producer Jack Good telling how excited he was when Gene Vincent first came to this country to do his television show, and instead of this dark rock 'n' roll monster, coming off the plane was a very polite southern gentleman with a very slight limp. Good then persuaded him to dress in leather and exaggerate the limp. It struck me as an early example of rock 'n' roll myth-making. . . . **Peter Gabriel**

It's no longer sex, drugs, and rock 'n' roll. It's crack, masturbation, and Madonna. So this [performing onstage in KISS makeup and clothing] was a way to live out our grade-school sexual rock 'n' roll fantasy.

Weiland, Stone Temple Pilots

This group The Sex Pistols pukes onstage? I don't necessarily like that. That's not showmanship. . . . They gotta get themselves an act. **Bo Diddley**

I can't use right-handed instruments now, because I snipped the ends of my fingers off. **Tony Iommi**, Black Sabbath

I smash guitars, because I like them. **Pete Townshend**

The better the singer's voice, the harder it is to believe what they're saying, so I used my faults to an advantage. **David Byrne**

I'm not trying to sell sex. I just don't like wearing a lot of clothes onstage.
Sheila E.

I'm not riding on The Beatles coattails. If they go, I'm going to be ready for the next person that comes along. **Murray the K**

Most videos are pretty much an insult to people's intelligence.
Joe Jackson

Some American kid recognized who I was and he says, "Your dad eats cows' heads." My daughter says, "You don't, Daddy. I've never seen you eat a cow's head." I thought that was kind of sweet. **Ozzy Osbourne**

. . . I know that if someone's purpose is to shock me, there's no way in the world they can shock me; if the performer's purpose is to unnerve me, then boy, I'm annoyed! **Paul Simon**

We've got to the stage where we end the night by destroying everything, which is expensive. **Pete Townshend**, circa 1967

My show is no-patter, no-dancing. If I scuttled all over the stage and went crazy, they'd say, "What's THAT all about?" **Roy Orbison**

Rock 'n' roll is simply an attitude. You don't have to play the greatest guitar.
Johnny Thunders, The New York Dolls

The only reason we wore sunglasses onstage was because we couldn't stand the sight of the audience.   **John Cale**, The Velvet Underground

[On Mick Jagger, Tina Turner, Dolly Parton, and other outrageous figures]: The trick is to caricature yourself and keep some kind of cool.
Marianne Faithfull

HISTORY

Rock 'n' roll is part of a pest to undermine the morals of the youth of our nation. It is sexualistic, unmoralistic, and ... brings people of both races together.   **North Alabama White Citizens Council**, 1950s

It's got a good beat. You can dance to it. I like the words. I'll give it a ninety-eight.   **Bobby**, 14, "American Bandstand," 1958

I sat down one night and wrote the line, "Rock, rock, rock, everybody." I was going to use the word "stomp," like, "Rock, rock, rock, and then stomp, stomp, stomp." But that didn't fit. I went from one word to another, and finally came up with "roll." It fit, because it was R and R, you know, two Rs. So the lyric went, "Rock, rock, rock everybody, roll, roll, roll everybody." So I finished the tune.... I asked Alan Freed to plug the record, and as the record was playing over the air, he would pound the desk. He would open the tune, pounding the desk and yelling over the record, "Rock everybody, roll everybody, rock 'n' roll!" Alan should be given credit for the name, but it came from a song that I wrote. That's the way it was.

Bill Haley (of the Comets)

Rock 'n' roll might best be summed up as monotony tinged with hysteria.
Vance Packard, author of *The Hidden Persuaders*, in testimony to the Senate Subcommittee on Interstate Commerce, 1958

Rock was born in a flashback, a celluloid loop doubled back inside a time machine. The date was 1954; the place was Cleveland, Ohio; the occasion, the first broadcast of Negro race records to an audience of white teenagers.
Arthur Goldman, *New American Review*, April, 1968

Rock 'n' roll was two pegs below a prison of war back then.
Ronnie Hawkins

Rock 'n' roll does for music what a motorcycle club at full throttle does for a quiet afternoon. The results bear passing resemblance to Hitler mass meetings. *Time*, 1956

Reeling like a top, snapping his fingers, and jerking his eyeballs, with hair like something Medusa had sent back, and a voice that was enormously improved by total unintelligibility.   **John Crosby**, about Fabian, 1960

When it comes to the minds and hairdos of our young people, something had to be done.

George Bush, on the CIA investigation of the "highly suspect" number of British rock bands signed to American contracts

The white youth of today have begun to react to the fact that the American way of life is a fossil of history. . . . All they know is that it feels good to swing to way-out body rhythms instead of drag-assing across the dance floor like zombies to the dead beat of mind-smothering Mickey Mouse music.

Eldridge Cleaver

A lot of people say Jerry Lee Lewis done wrong, but that has yet to be proven in the eyes of God.   **Jerry Lee Lewis**

In England, when rock 'n' roll happened, it was different than it was in the States, where you had all the basic ingredients if you wanted to find them. . . . But in England, it just suddenly—Boom!—one minute it wasn't there and suddenly it was Little Richard and Elvis and Chuck Berry.

Keith Richards

It was like being in the eye of a hurricane. You'd wake up in a concert and think, "Wow, how did I get here?"   **John Lennon**

The Mersey Sound is the voice of eighty thousand crumbling houses and thirty thousand people on the dole. *The Daily Worker*, 1963

I can't say "fuck" on a record. Fuck is a nice word. Fuck means something pretty. I like fuck. And I can't say it on a record. **David Crosby**, 1960s

HYPE

... Hype and deception go with the music; man, they go with the music.
Andrew Loog Oldham, manager, The Rolling Stones

My fantasy (guitar) would be a cannon that shot sperm at the audience.
Angus Young, AC/DC

The Grateful Dead should be sponsored by the government—a public service. And they should set us up to play at places that need to get high.
Jerry Garcia

You have official Urge permission to make up our quotes.
Blackie Onassis, Urge Overkill

I wouldn't say we have a publicity strategy for this tour. The Stones, we believe, make their own news.

David Horowitz, publicist for The Stones' American tour, 1969

[On accusations that the classic album *London Calling* by The Clash represented a "sell-out" because of its use of more diverse and melodic musical forms]: When I read that, the notion was so new to me I just laughed. In that dirty room in Pimlico, with one light and filthy carpet on the walls for soundproofing, that had been the furthest thought from our minds.

Joe Strummer

Ultimately, I want to make everybody horny.   **Patti Smith**

I don't pretend to give a message of any kind, except enjoy yourself and get laid.   **Lemmy**, Motörhead

I will personally cut off my dick and eat it! I will cut my cock off on "The Ed Sullivan Show" and chew on it. This is what I'll do if the new album bombs.   **Ted Nugent**

[On why The Sex Pistols failed to appear as scheduled on "Saturday Night Live"]: It's very strange that a group that prides itself on representing the underground turns us down because we don't pay them enough.

Lorne Michaels, "Saturday Night Live" producer, 1977

We're the McDonald's of rock. We're always there to satisfy, and a billion served.   **Paul Stanley**, KISS

[Their manager on the early days of The Rolling Stones]: . . . I'd stand in the back, and when the Stones got rolling, I'd start squealing in a high pitch, and that would set off all the little girls. Nothing is as contagious as a good squeal. That's what the media picked up as "spontaneous enthusiasm."

Andrew Oldham

At home, sometimes I just like to watch TV. I enjoy good detective stories, something that engages your mind. Not violent shows, though. I don't like to watch too much violence.   **Ike Turner**

I think the Sex Pistols have copped out. Now they're on the front of *Rolling Stone*. That's a real cop-out.   **Mick Jagger**

[His response when asked by critic Timothy White if the brevity of The Ramones songs was tongue-in-cheek, a gimmick]: The what of the song was what?   **Johnny Ramone**

IMAGE

Rock 'n' roll is not so much a question of electric guitars as it is striped pants.
David Lee Roth

I think it's an asset to a performer to be sexually attractive.
Carly Simon

L.A.'s okay, I guess, if you wanna be the bronzed goddess driving around in your Cherokee Jeep in your satin shorts, with your asshole rock 'n' roll star boyfriend with his shorts full of cocaine. . . .
Chrissie Hynde, 1981

We [John Lennon, Yoko Ono] always sang a lot. . . . Finally, Yoko would say, "Do the one that I like—do my favorite one." That was "The Way We Were" from the Streisand/Redford movie. Gosh! Did they love that movie! John had his hair cut like Robert Redford.
Elliot Mintz

It's very easy to presume that I'm not a human being.
Frank Zappa

We always hated being called an art band. I never took art in high school.
Thurston Moore, Sonic Youth

They think we're satanic.   **Kurt Cobain**

Nowadays, we're more into staying in our rooms and reading Nietzsche.
                                                             Jimmy Page

We just did our own thing, which was a combination of rock 'n' roll, and
Fellini, and game-show host, and corn, and mysticism.
                                                    Fred Schneider, B-52s

I'm trying to be a public figure, and at the same time be average. It's like
proclaiming my ordinariness.   **James Taylor**

We like to look sixteen and bored shitless.   **David Johansen**

If I'm considered part of that overhyped, overproduced, overindulgent super-
group style, then I'm bummed.   **Billy Joel**

The Sex Pistols are like some contagious disease.   **Malcolm McLaren**

[On how The Ramones overcame a vastly unsuccessful criminal past]: We
got into a group, and we became nice.   **Johnny Ramone**

What is evil? I don't know how much people think of Mick [Jagger] as the
Devil or just a good rock performer. There are black musicians who think
we are acting as unknown agents of Lucifer, and others who think we are
Lucifer. Everybody's Lucifer.   **Keith Richards**

Time Out asked me if I'm a committed drag queen or not, which pissed me off. Committed? What's committed? How can you be committed to a pair of falsies and stilettos?
                                                                    Boy George

There is something elegantly sinister about The Rolling Stones. They sit before you at a press conference like five unfolding switchblades; their faces set in rehearsed snarls; their hair studiously unkempt and matted; their clothes part of some private conceit; and the way they walk and they talk and the songs they sing all become part of some long mean reach for the jugular.
                                                                    Pete Hamill

I always like sort of funny, corny, pompous stage names, like Iggy Pop and Billy Idol. My father suggested Black Francis; it's an old family name.
                                                                    Frank Black

I think Mick Jagger would be astounded and amazed if he realized to many people he is not a sex symbol, but a mother image.   **David Bowie**

INSPIRATION

It's been very important throughout my life career that I've met all the guys I've copied, because at each stage they've said, "Don't play like me, play like you."   **Eric Clapton**

I am the strings, and the Supreme is the musician.   **Carlos Santana**

People lead really flat lives. They need a sort of peak. I like to be that peak.   **Michael Hutchence**, INXS

Handicaps are really to be used another way—to benefit yourself and others.   **Stevie Wonder**

When I was twelve or thirteen, I would do things like set the alarm clock for midnight, and I'd get up very quietly and put on my trench coat. I'd sneak downstairs to the living room with a spyglass, look through the keyhole, and keep a notebook on, say, [older sister] "Joey's date with Mark." I'd make a list of things I'd see or hear. . . . Since then, I've always felt that a lot of my songs deal with spying on myself.   **Carly Simon**

Let me describe one of the biggest musical influences of my life. It was Sly and the Family Stone's "Hot Fun in the Summertime." I was only three years old when that song had me jumping up and down.... There's also The Turtles's "Happy Together" and The Association's "Windy" and Simon and Garfunkel's "Feelin' Groovy." Those are all precious moments to me.

Janet Jackson

I believe in the power of the spoken word.   **Anita Baker**

We were born to struggle, to face the challenges of our lifetime, and, ultimately, to evolve to a higher consciousness.   **Quincy Jones**

Three things I never wanted to own: a dog, a cane, a guitar. In my mind, they each mean blindness and helplessness.   **Ray Charles**

[On recording his hit solo album *Empty Glass*]: In a way, I've got the punk explosion to thank for making that decision. It freed me. It allowed me to be myself. It dignified me, in a way, to be cast to one side. I felt uneasy with the way The Who were inevitably on the road to mega-stardom.... [It] was the most important thing I've ever done for me—to allow me to have a new beginning and to actually grow.   **Pete Townshend**

I really love Americans and American musical roots. It could be my British need for discipline that makes me admire the American appetite for freedom and passion.   **Steve Winwood**

I have to really feel a song before I'll deal with it; and just about every song I do is based either on an experience I've had or an experience someone I know had gone through. **Aretha Franklin**

INSULTS

The majority of pop stars are complete idiots in every respect. **Sade**

Groups like Genesis and Yes are about as exciting as used Kleenex. It might as well be Tony Bennett. **Nick Lowe**

Led Zeppelin is just a bunch of stupid idiots who wrote cool riffs.
Chris Cornell, Soundgarden

[On the now-legendary Velvet Underground]: It will replace nothing, except maybe suicide. **Cher**

[On Tiffany]: . . . She hasn't got a look, and she's got a dumpy body and no talent that I can see. **Dave Mustaine**, Megadeth

A sobering thought: A century from now what we know as modern music will be considered old-fashioned. This thought almost makes one reconciled to the possibility that there may not be any twenty-first century.

Frank Sullivan, Irish-American comedian

. . . Liverpool never produced a decent musician and The Beatles were living proof of it. **Ian Stewart**

We've never been darlings of the press. In fact, I remember reading one article that said we were the only band that was uglier than Los Lobos. So I went and checked out the movie *La Bamba*, and saw Los Lobos at the end, and I said, "Huh-uh, no way." People may think we're ugly but we're not THAT ugly. **Mike Muir**, Suicidal Tendencies

People look to the people at the top, and the people at the top universally are assholes. **Pete Townshend**

Mick Jagger has child-bearing lips. **Joan Rivers**

Music is like girlfriends to me; I'm continually astonished by the choices other people make. **David Lee Roth**

In England, you know you can become famous for doing absolutely nothing. . . . London is the only city in the world that is run entirely on bullshit. **Boy George**

Seeing or not
seeing, life is still
life. I don't need to
see to play or sing
the way I do. That
comes from within.

Ray Charles

The Who and The Stones are revolting. All they're good for is making money.
John Lydon (née Johnny Rotten), 1986

Sting was boring and pretentious. Everyone was driven to distraction by his endless speeches on political matters.   **Kathleen Turner**, actress

A lot of big bands in the States seem to be frighteningly ignorant of stuff that is really their own heritage. They have this rock and this heavy metal music in America that doesn't have any roots in rock 'n' roll and soul or anything. It's a creation of the 1970s. I'm talking about the Totos and the Rushes— those groups that sing, "We're a rock 'n' roll band!" or "We're rocking tonight!" And they don't have anything to do with rock 'n' roll, and wouldn't know it if it bit them.   **Elvis Costello**

Nothing is capable of being well-set to music that is not nonsense.
Anonymous

Artists like U2 and Bruce Springsteen who are more directly linked to me, I find very wanting.   **Pete Townshend**

Mick Jagger is a scared little boy who is about as sexy as a pissing toad. He moves like a parody between a majorette girl and Fred Astaire.
Truman Capote

New York? Who'd want to live there? It's like living on top of a rotting corpse, vampire life. You crawl out of your coffin and go into the decaying streets— and get shot at.   **John Hiatt**

THE LEGENDS

I may be a living legend, but that sure don't help when I've got to change a flat tire.   **Roy Orbison**

He's the king of rock 'n' roll.   **Jerry Lee Lewis's Mom**, on Chuck Berry

People aren't supposed to be like me, sing like me, live like me, but now they're paying me fifty thousand dollars a year for me to be like me.
Janis Joplin

I'm the one that's got to die when it's time for me to die, so let me live my life the way I want to.   **Jimi Hendrix**

They call me Lady Soul, so let me tell you something about soul. Soul is something creative, something active. Soul is honesty. I sing to people about what matters. I sing to the realists; people who accept it like it is. I express problems. There are tears when it's sad and smiles when it's happy. It seems simple to me, but to some, feelings take courage.

Aretha Franklin

As far as I'm concerned, there won't be a Beatles reunion as long as John Lennon remains dead.   **George Harrison**

With John [Lennon], there was an element of fear. He really quite frightened people, including me in the beginning, because of his attitude. He was rough-ready and not my type at all, to start with. But this enigmatic character you couldn't resist.   **Cynthia Lennon**

He was my husband. He was my lover. He was my friend. He was my partner. And he was an old soldier who fought with me.

Yoko Ono, on John Lennon

If I'm going to hell, I'm going there playing the piano.   **Jerry Lee Lewis**

I saw rock 'n' roll future, and its name is Bruce Springsteen.

Jon Landau, music critic, former manager to Bruce Springsteen

Growing up the son of a Beatle didn't seem any different to me as a kid. It was the people around me that made me notice that there was something different. It was hard to understand why people would like me more or dislike me for having a famous father. I didn't understand about the fame. It was difficult, but it was a learning thing.   **Julian Lennon**

I was having a lot of flashbacks when Axl [Rose] came into the studio, because I know how it felt when I was twenty or twenty-three and went in to sing on other people's records who'd been doing it for a long time. I was scared to death sometimes, but I also had a lotta nerve—and so does he. He stood out there and sang for hours, until he got a migraine headache. We had to make him stop singing. His voice is like a chainsaw. **Don Henley**

Quite simply, I feel that the Stones are the world's best rock 'n' roll band.
Pete Townshend

Onstage, I make love to twenty-five thousand people, then I go home alone.
Janis Joplin

They call me "the Godfather of Soul." None of the new generation can ever be Godfather. The only people that qualify are myself and Sinatra.
James Brown

Bob Dylan is the closest thing to a saint that I know of among white people in America. **Nina Simone**

Alan Freed jumped into radio like a stripper into Swan Lake. He was a teenager's mind funneled into fifty thousand watts.
Chuck Whelton, *The New York Times*

The first time I sat in with Lightnin' [Hopkins], I was intimidated. It was difficult to fall into the groove with him, even though I knew all his stuff; you just needed to feel it. I got through playing and I sat down at this table, and I didn't know Lightnin' was sitting right behind me. This guy asks, "How does it feel playing with Hopkins?" And I said, "It's great, but it doesn't feel like he's changing at the right points." Lightnin' tapped me on the shoulder and said, "Lightnin' change when Lightnin' want to." **Dusty Hill**

People at school told me I couldn't make it, that I would end up making potholders.   **Stevie Wonder**

You see the sun making an appearance. It's absolutely silent. But the power it projects! The heat, the light, the radiation is so vast, so powerful.
                                        Alice Coltrane, remembering John Coltrane

Ringo played the backbeat and never got off it. Man, you couldn't have moved him with a crane.   **D.J. Fontana**

[On husband Frank]: He probably scared the shit out of his mother, too.
                                                                Gail Zappa

A singer really was the last thing I wanted to be.   **David Bowie**

Speaking for myself, I looked on the band [The Rolling Stones] as a way to practice, and I never seriously considered that we'd ever get to actually perform anywhere.   **Ian Stewart**

I'm not afraid to be the boss, see? That's how James Brown music came to be. Back when everybody was listening to soapsuds songs and jingles, I emphasized the beat, not the melody, unnerstand? Heat the beat and the rest'll turn sweet.   **James Brown**

I never considered myself the greatest, but I'm the best. **Jerry Lee Lewis**

If you take a black left hand and a white right hand and put them together, you've got rock 'n' roll. And that's Jerry Lee.

Jim McBride, director of the film *Great Balls of Fire*

Sly Stone, James Brown, these are people that started funky music. They stood between the gospelly soul and the dance music. And that's funk: Sly, James Brown, and people like that. Wilson Picket, Otis Redding. And of course in rock 'n' roll, there's Little Richard and Chuck Berry and all those guys. That's who I would always watch. And Jackie Wilson—yeow!

Michael Jackson

[On producing Aretha Franklin for the album *Who's Zoomin' Who?*]: She's a black Mae West. She's very fast. I didn't pull anything out of her. She's so vast and brings so much to her takes that it's more of a question of keeping up with her. And when it stops, it stops. So you've got to be on your toes. Before any session with her, I'd jog four or five miles just to be mentally alert. You have to be—she's the queen.

Narada Michael Walden, Mahavishnu Orchestra

[On the chart success of Bowie's "Let's Dance"]: David might not want to say this, but for the first few weeks, even he was surprised. He's a big artist and a rock 'n' roll demigod, but there was still a garage-band guy in there who couldn't believe his record was selling. I'd be lying in bed, and the phone would ring: "Hello, Nile? This is David. Look what's happening, did you see *Billboard* this week? Wow, unbelievable!" **Nile Rodgers**, producer

[After being corrected on his pronunciation of the name of Atlantic Records legend Ahmet Ertegun]: I thought they called him Omelet 'cause he likes to eat omelets, the way they call a cat Hamhocks who eats hamhocks.

Otis Redding

I've known Mr. [James] Brown since I was fifteen or sixteen, hanging around the back fence of the mansion he useta have in Queens. He had a castle with a moat around it on Linden Boulevard in the St. Albans section of Queens, and the kids from my neighborhood in the Hollis section of the borough would go over to look at the giant concrete gold "Please, Please, Please" record he had imbedded in his front yard. There was a lot of big shots living on that street, but he was the only one who'd come out and tell us to stay in school. It was inspirational.　**Reverend Al Sharpton, Jr.**

There's never much time goes by that I don't think of him [Buddy Holly].
Waylon Jennings [Jennings lost his seat in a coin toss on the doomed plane flight that killed his good friend and mentor.]

[On The Beatles]: The thing was we meet and shake hand and say great—them dude they nice. I really like meet them and sit down and chat with them. They're bredrens. Jah just love roots. Them guys are roots. Them guys are all right, ya know.　**Bob Marley**

DAGMAR

[On Who mate,
Pete Townshend]:
He's talked himself
up his own arse.

Roger Daltrey

THE LIFE

Rock 'n' roll is the lowest form of life known to man.   **Elvis Costello**

I just can't believe that anyone would start a band just to make the scene and be cool and have chicks.   **Kurt Cobain**

I thought being in a band was an antiestablishment lifestyle. It's only ever been my interest to maintain that, and to maintain my freedom as a bum. I don't want to be recognized; I don't want to be hassled. I just want to play guitar in a rock 'n' roll band.   **Chrissie Hynde**

Old at heart, but I'm only twenty-eight.   **Axl Rose**

[On the demise of The Sex Pistols and the start of his new band, Public Image Ltd.]: I don't want to live in history books. We're trying to write the next chapter.   **John Lydon** (née Johnny Rotten)

I feel old for some reason. I really feel like an old soul.

Michael Jackson

Most of these young bands did not have to break the paths D.O.A. or Black Flag did, where you would play and go to the club owner, say, "Can we have our money?" and he would hold a billy club and say, "Let's fight for it."

Henry Rollins

It's not like being in band is all that fun or anything.

J. Mascis, Dinosaur Jr.

Basically, rock 'n' roll is all about looking good, living fast, and dying young.

Joe Jackson

I wouldn't like in fifteen years time to still be playing "Crocodile Rock."

Elton John

Keith [Moon] was a very positive musician, a very positive performer, but a very negative animal. He needed you for his act—on and off stage.

Pete Townshend

LIFE BEFORE ROCK

When I was in school in the first grade, the teacher told me, she said one and one was two. I said, now wait a minute, how do you know? And right then we had a big problem.   **Jerry Lee Lewis**

I played the piano in church. I even taught bible school one year. Then I got into the greatest gospel hits of the 70s, and it was all over.   **Axl Rose**

One of the biggest memories of my life—the biggest—is stealing home in the bottom of the eleventh inning of a high school baseball game when I was sixteen years old.... I truly believe that was it, and don't think I've done anything greater since.   **Paul Simon**

I was a Future Farmer of America, yeah—F.F.A. It had another name, but we can't go into that.   **Don Henley**

... I hope I never forget that incredible time of evolving from a girl into a woman. You start wearing hair curlers, and your breasts are growing, and you're climbing up into some tree to kiss some boy.... It's so important to always keep that innocence.   **Ricki Lee Jones**

I was a punk in the fifties. **Joni Mitchell**

Whenever my mother went to work, my older sister took care of us, and wherever she went, we had to go—including choir practice. I was the only boy in a choir of thirty-six girls, because to sing in a choir was considered sissy. **Billy Ocean**

I went into the closet and said, "I'm gonna kill myself." There was chlorine bleach and I said, "Nah, that's gonna taste bad." So I took the Pledge. All I ended up doing was farting furniture polish.

Billy Joel, recalling his youth

I used to dress up and pretend to be a rock star when I was a kid, but now the words "rock star" don't even exist in my vocabulary.

Kip Winger, member of Winger

I started playing clarinet, but the orthodontist said I was going to have a bad overbite and that I'd better quit, so I found a ukulele.... But Daddy said, "The only two big ukulele guys I can think of are Ukulele Ike and Arthur Godfrey.... You'd better try guitar." **Johnny Winter**

We were Poor. I'm spelling it with a capital P.... We were on the bottom of the ladder looking up at everyone else. Nothing below us 'cept the ground.

Ray Charles

I used to take accordion lessons. I whipped out some heavy polkas and Beatles tunes n' shit. **Tommy Lee, Mötley Crüe**

When we were in high school, we were the only people that even played music, I mean rock.

Tom Fogerty

LOVE

Sometimes a woman can really persuade you to make an asshole of yourself.

Rod Stewart

I don't think you can look for love. All you can do is get yourself in a situation where you don't discourage something that may be rather nice.

Linda Ronstadt

The memory of love is a powerful thing; it's a tangible possession in and of itself, and I guess that's been a theme running through my whole personal development as well as my career.

Bob Seger

You can have the number one album, number one selling automobile, or whatever, but if you don't have somebody to run home to and jump up and down about it, then it's pretty empty.

Anita Baker

[On the early days of his marriage to Tina Turner]: When we were together, she was so kind and sweet and understanding. You just don't know. In those days, she was like a thousand percent in my corner. I mean, if I said to her, "Go and shoot that guy!" she'd shoot him without even thinking whether it was right or wrong. We were that tight.
Ike Turner

Tina Turner

I had the worst crush on the "God of Thunder" Gene Simmons. They appealed to me because they're really basic. Plus they're so evil!

Kat Bjelland, groupie of KISS

Just say that I'm still searching for an angel with a broken wing. It's not very easy to find them these days.   **Jimmy Page**

[On his romance with singer Suzzy Roche]: Okay, I confess. I do have this thing about Catholic singing sisters with dark hair who make records for Warner Brothers.   **Loudon Wainwright III**, folk musician

Love is never ending. Love is always.   **Smokey Robinson**

THE MAGIC'S IN THE MUSIC

Magic is what we do. Music is the way we do it.   **Jerry Garcia**

The true musician is to bring light into people's hearts. If I can bring joy into the world, if I can get people to stop thinking about their pain for a moment, or the fact that tomorrow morning they're going to get up and tell their boss off—if I can delay that for a moment and bring a little joy into that spot and help them to see things a little bit differently, then I'll be successful.

Anonymous

Music allowed me to eat. But it also allowed me to express myself. I played because I had to play. I rid myself of bad dreams and rotten memories.

Prince

Rock 'n' roll starts between the legs and goes through the heart, then to the head. As long as it does those three things, it's a great rock song.

John Cougar Mellencamp

Close your eyes as I take you on the experience of my life, the experience of hearing many different sounds from many different cultures from around the world. We hear the energy, the sound of music, the sound of someone saying, "I love you."

Stevie Wonder

For me, music is this magic acoustic element that makes perfectly rational people, who have come to realize the unalterable fact that they are truly alone in this world, somehow feel for fleeting moments that maybe they're not after all. . . . It's a chemical reaction of some sort. A very odd thing.

Billy Joel

When we did *Sgt. Pepper*, we were just given a license to kill, so to speak, because we were already successful. And I knew that I could go in the studio and do just what I wanted; and I knew that they wanted to experiment a bit more. So we just let our hair down and went for broke.

George Martin, producer

I believe my music is the healin' music. I believe my music can make the blind see, the lame walk, the deaf and dumb hear and talk, because it inspires and uplifts people. It regenerates the heart, makes the liver quiver, the bladder splatter, and the knees freeze. I'm not conceited, either.

Little Richard

Music is my addiction. When I get into it, I just fly.

Philip Michael Thomas

Sounds like the blues are composed of feeling, finesse, and fear.

Billy Gibbons

. . . Once you get rolling, there's no problem. What's good for the music will be good for us personally.   **Keith Richards**

I believe it's no good to talk about your songs; it's wrong. You should leave your songs alone and let them say what they say; let people take what they want from them.   **Paul Simon**

If I told you what our music is really about, we'd probably all get arrested.

Bob Dylan

Soul is howling at the moon—and having the moon respond.

Daryl Hall

I think people who can truly live a life in music are telling the world, "You can have my love, you can have my smiles. Forget the bad parts, you don't need them. Just take the music, the goodness, because it's the very best and it's the part I give most willingly." **George Harrison**

[On the last stages of putting together his 1989 album *New York*]: We had tried to put songs in order, to tell the story moodwise and emotionally. And when it didn't work, it was so bad it was unbelievable. Then Victor [Deyglio], one of the engineers, said, "There's a trick I've learned over the years. Why not put it in the order that it was recorded in?" And there it was. Wow!

Lou Reed

Music is forever; music should grow and mature with you, following you right on up until you die. **Paul Simon**

There's never been logic to music being forgotten, for if a song is good, it should be good all the time. You never throw away a book that's good. And music should be treated as well. **Phil Everly**

We play the machines, but the machines also play us. This we don't deny like they do in conventional music. There the man is always considered superior to his machine, but this is not so. The machine should not only do slave work. We try to treat them as colleagues so they exchange energies with us. **Ralf Hütter**, Kraftwerk

Music should never be harmless.   **Robbie Robertson**

I'll go back to bars before I ever go commercial, because it's important to keep this music alive.   **Stevie Ray Vaughan**

It's all in the songs. If you've got the songs, it's all very simple.

Tom Petty

If it makes you move, or moves you, or grooves you, it'll be here; the blues rolls on, rock steady knocks, and they all are here now, and I think they all will be here from now on.   **Chuck Berry**

MARKETING

The [Rolling] Stones aren't playing rock 'n' roll anymore. They are playing for Budweiser.   **Mike O'Connell**, member of Mike and the Mechanics

If you wanna sell records, I'm told, you gotta make videos. I know they're thought of as an art form, but I don't think they are.... When I saw the video, all I saw was a shot of me from my mouth to my forehead on the screen. I figure, isn't that something? I'm paying for that?

Bob Dylan

[On using rock songs in commercials]: If I was being a purist, I'd say no one should give the songs to ads. My heart says that. But, you know, you're not always as pure as you think.

Paul McCartney

It's irrelevant whether Michael Jackson drinks Pepsi or Duran Duran drinks Coke. What's relevant is what these groups stand for and what their sponsors hope to stand for by tying in with them.

Allen Rosenbine, chairman BBDO

Don't try to explain it; just sell it.   **Colonel Tom Parker**

Grunge is a really neat word. It was a good marketing term; it has a nice ring to it.   **Anonymous**

In the sixties, rock was a scary proposition in most corporate boardrooms. It became the antithesis of materialism and the corporate American way. But in the eighties, that no longer holds true.

Danny Socolof, president, MEGA

I think of what we do as the equivalent of working at Lockheed. Writing songs is being in research and development, making records is production, and going out on tour is sales. We're going out to sell our B-1 bomber.

Anonymous

I don't set trends. I just find out what they are and exploit them.

Dick Clark

I don't cross over. I expand. I'm expanding my market just like any other business. I don't know of one business that caters only to one people. If they did, most of the businesses would go bankrupt.   **Hammer**

I don't want my album coming out with a G rating. Nobody would buy it.
Donny Osmond, reacting to the Parents' Music Resource Center

The business we are in is the advertising business, and that's the only business any radio station should be in.
Dave Shepperd, DRES, Moberly, Missouri

MATERIALISM

Somebody said to me, "But The Beatles were antimaterialistic." That's a huge myth. John and I literally used to sit down and say, "Now, let's write a swimming pool." **Paul McCartney**

Everything you buy is an added burden. **Billy Ocean**

Nothing in what I got out of Guns N' Roses monetarily or famewise, I could really give a shit about. It was, and is always, the band. If . . . GN'R suddenly ended, I'd be in serious fucking trouble because I depend on them.
Slash

I'm in House of Lords for a few reasons. One for the money, two for the money, and three for the money!   **Chuck Wright**

If you're worshipping things, it means you're not really leading a full life. It's healthy to admire; all of my musical growth has come out of admiration. But to worship, that's taking it too far. You've got to get yourself together if you do that.   **Joni Mitchell**

MONEY

... That kind of popularity wasn't the reason we originally organized The Stones. We were real serious; we were evangelists at that time. It was a very pure sort of idealistic, adolescent drive that kept us going. The money, we didn't give a damn about the money—at that age, who cares? That wasn't the point. The point was to spread the music.   **Keith Richards**

Of course we're doing it for the money as well. . . . We've always done it for the money.   **Mick Jagger**

Money mon-monee! Is plenty things them people don't know, you know. Is plenty wisdom them people don't know. Because is few guys know that figures ain't got no end. You can start all over again. Numbers. They don't go more than nine. But they don't have no end. That means, if numbers is where you get your kicks from—to have plenty—then you're lost. Because it don't have no end. So plenty people don't realize that this thing is something happening here. This shit don't have no end. Ya know. It's just madness. Weirdness. Weird situation. **Bob Marley**

[After being asked if The Rolling Stones were reuniting only to cash in]: No, that's The Who. **Ron Wood**

[About an encounter with James Brown]: He read me the cash receipts from his last tour, and then he broke out into the aisle, sliding and doing the James Brown dance. And then he walked off. **Michael Jackson**

I think I'm lucky I didn't get paid enough to drown in the syrup of success. **Iggy Pop**

I think Mick's main ambition as a boy was to be rich. Money meant a lot to him. **Chris Jagger**, Mick's brother

It [money] just means you have different problems to deal with. And it brings its own problems. Like "Who are you going to put on retainer?"
Keith Richards

PERFORMING LIVE

I'll go on any tour. I got to sing "Knockin' on Heaven's Door" with Bob [Dylan] and Tom [Petty]! I'll never forget in my life walking out to perform, and having Bob Dylan turn and do a little bow. It made everything all right—all the pain, all the trouble, all the hassles that come along with this kind of life in rock 'n' roll. They all went away at that moment.   **Stevie Nicks**

Joseph Campbell labelled me a conjurer one night. He was watching us play and said, "What you are is a conjurer." I thought about it for a coupla months and decided, "Yeah, you're right."   **Bob Weir**

I'm probably going deaf from it, but it's truly electrifying. It's not an ego thing like, "Hey, aren't we superhuman?" It's more sexual. Somebody makes a lot of noise, indicating how much they enjoy what you're doing. You get revved up, you perform a little better—fingernails on the back, the whole nine yards. I'm a child of the sixties. But what I want the music to do—uplift, unite, create a bond—hasn't changed.   **Billy Joel**

... My own preferences are for improvisation, for making it up as I go along. The idea of picking, of eliminating possibilities by deciding, that's difficult for me.   **Jerry Garcia**

The first time I was at the Apollo, I threw my tie out to them, and they threw it back to me. I said, "James, you have got some work to do."

James Brown

Onstage, I've been hit by a grapefruit, beer cans, eggs, spit, money, cigarette butts, mandies, quaaludes, joints, bras, panties, and a fist. **Iggy Pop**

I actually went deaf for a period of time. **Eric Clapton**

I'm still that sort to let them wet their knickers on the seats. That's basically what it's all about for me. **Cliff Richard**

Nobody could ever hear us anyway. There was always too much noise.

Mark Lindsay, Paul Revere and the Raiders

When I get onstage, I don't know what happens, honest to God. It feels so good, it's like the safest place in the world. **Michael Jackson**

I thank you in advance for the great round of applause I am about to get.

Bo Diddley

Some of the things I used to see from the stage! You'd probably think it was nothing, but this woman, one of the stripteasers, would take her drawers off, and men would come up to her and they'd start doing—aw, man! She was too funky! That, to me, was awful. **Michael Jackson**

The guys are there to make the broads, the broads are just sittin' there waitin' for the guys, and I'm up there on the bandstand makin' my guitar.

Link Wray

If we stay in small clubs, we'll develop small minds, and then we'll develop small music.   **Bono**

We go home safe in the knowledge that we've deafened a few.

Phil Taylor, Motörhead

Rock 'n' roll is to me ... just sort of funny entertainment. Mass funny entertainment. There is a certain basic element in the form which is agreeable, especially performing it in sports arenas. It's like an art un-event. I prefer that to the Metropolitan Opera House.   **Mick Jagger**

What I got kicked out of school for, it's the same thing that I see myself doing onstage now. It's just a lot of high-powered feelings, a lot of emotion, and now I can work it to my advantage. The same thing I got hired for, I got fired for.   **Ricki Lee Jones**

I'd like to say that we're not boring. We play great music and we're exciting. We jump about and wiggle our bums.   **Joe Strummer**

Sometimes an orgasm is better than being onstage. Sometimes being onstage is better than an orgasm.   **Mick Jagger**

It's the most over-milked, watered-down bullshit I've ever seen, this damn encore stuff.
Frank Black

PHILOSOPHY

A musician should be as much a part of a community as a bricklayer or a shopkeeper.
Stuart Adamson, Big Country

My role in society, or any artist or poet's role, is to try and express what we all feel. Not to tell people how to feel. Not as a preacher, not as a leader, but as a reflection of us all.
John Lennon

You can't look forward and backward at the same time.
Coleman Young

You must have the Devil in you to succeed in any of the arts.
Voltaire

I've come to realize that life is not a musical comedy, it's a Greek tragedy.
Billy Joel

But in truth, there's only three types of people in the world: people who work, people who are not allowed to, and people who don't have to.

Elvis Costello

We all have ability. The difference is how we use it.   **Stevie Wonder**

From the day you're born till the day you ride in a hearse, there's nothing so bad.   **Smokey Robinson**

No matter how big or soft or warm your bed is, you still have to get out of it.   **Grace Slick**

I'm certainly enjoying life, I will say that. I could learn to relax more. You know, if you're gonna hold a bird, you have to hold it with a certain tension, or it will fly away. But if you crush it, you're gonna kill it. I gotta learn how to hold the bird.   **Iggy Pop**

I remember there was a riot there. People were fighting, the kids were fighting. . . . The policeman asked us, "Where do you come from?" I said, "We come from singing." They said, "You are singing while the people are fighting?" I said, "Yes. They are doing their job. I am doing mine."

Joseph Shabalala, Ladysmith Black Mambazo

Rock music is a necessary step in the evolution of man, as was LSD, Hitler, the electric light, and everything else.   **Mel Lyman**

Here we are in the eighties, practically the nineties, talking about the same thing we were talking about in the thirties.   **James Brown**

Don't forget, the penis is mightier than the sword.
                                        Screamin' Jay Hawkins

If anything, rock 'n' roll should fit the proletarian view of art, which is partly what made punk so powerful.   **Jerry Harrison**, The Talking Heads

Life is what happens to you while you're busy making other plans.
                                                    John Lennon

To live is to suffer; to survive is to find some meaning in the suffering.
                                                    Roberta Flack

Marijuana took rock 'n' roll into the future, and rock 'n' roll took marijuana to the masses so they could climb into the future, too, and nobody's ever been the same since.   **John Sinclair**, activist

Great artists suffer for the people.   **Marvin Gaye**

An education opens a person's mind to the entire world. And there is nothing more important than to make sure everyone has the opportunity for an education.   **Michael Jackson**

I think pop music has done more for oral intercourse than anything else that ever happened, and vice versa.   **Frank Zappa**

Dad had a wonderful habit of talking to everybody the same way. A briefcase and a three-piece suit didn't impress him. "The guy with the mop may have the answer you need," my father told me, "but if you're holding your head too high, you're going to miss what he's saying."   **Lionel Ritchie**

The truth is where the truth is and sometimes it's in the candy store.
                                                        Keith Richards

The only thing that keeps half the people alive in factories is the fucking radio on all day.   **Johnny Rotten** (John Lydon)

Most fear stems from sin: To limit one's sins, one must assuredly limit one's fear, thereby bringing more peace to one's spirit.   **Marvin Gaye**

Music needs to make sense, needs to have order. From what some people consider the lowest stuff—a cat in the middle of a cotton field shouting the blues—to what's considered the highest—a symphony or an opera—it has to be structured.   **Ray Charles**

My mother taught me that my talent for singing and dancing was as much God's work as a beautiful sunset or a storm that left snow for children to play in.   **Michael Jackson**

Music has helped society accept gay sexuality, because of the weird creatures on TV—Boy George, Marilyn, Freddie Mercury.
                    Paul Rutherford, Frankie Goes to Hollywood

Courage is one step ahead of fear. **Coleman Young**

To me, people are more important than anything else. Rock 'n' roll, anything else, people are more important. **Keith Richards**

I take dreams very seriously. I think everyone should. **Peter Gabriel**

It is important to call your mom; it is important to tidy your room. It is important to make sure you don't have too many drinks and kill someone on the way home, or even scrape somebody's car. It's the little details that we have control of. **Pete Townshend**

Rock can be seen as one attempt to break out of this dead and soulless universe and reassert the universe of magic [sic].

William S. Burroughs, author

POLITICS

You can't trust politicians. It doesn't matter who makes a political speech. It's all lies ... and it applies to any rock star who wants to make a political speech as well.   **Bob Geldof**

I think politics is an instrument.   **Bob Dylan**

I don't even know what politics are, to tell you the truth.   **Bob Dylan**

Who wants politics in music? I find politics the single most uninspiring, unemotional, insensitive activity on this planet.   **Adam Ant**

Unlike Dr. King, U2 make pathetic preachers. That's not our job. And we're not on a speaking tour or a lecture tour, we're on a rock 'n' roll tour, hopefully making music that will inspire people to whatever they freely want to do, whether it's walk their girlfriend home or join Amnesty International. It's up to them. I like to think that maybe they can do both.   **Bono**

[Bruce Springsteen] is a national presence, his charisma co-opted by as unlikely an adherent as Ronald Reagan—even as Springsteen himself pokes relentlessly

G. A. B.

The system want pure love songs like ol' Frank Sinatra, they don't want not'ing wit' no protest. It makes too much trouble.

Bob Marley

through the withered and waterless cultural underbrush of the President's new American Eden.   **Kurt Loder**, *Rolling Stone*, 1984

Since every record released surely contains something offensive to someone, sticker them all. Make this as meaningless as the bar code.
    Michael Stipe, on placing warning labels on recordings

Politics is part of life, and you would be ignoring a whole aspect of life by leaving it out of songs.   **Bruce Cockburn**

Politicians are necessary, and it'd be foolish to blame them for our troubles. They're just doing what they've always done—looking to survive, looking to climb, trying to please everyone at once, and grinning and lying while they're doing it.   **Ray Charles**

Poverty makes people angry, brings out their worst side.   **Prince**

The Youth International Revolution will begin with a mass breakdown of authority.... Tribes of long hairs, blacks, armed women, peasants, and students will take over.... The White House will become one big commune.... The Pentagon will be replaced by an LSD experimental farm.... To steal from the rich is a sacred and religious act.
    Jerry Rubin, 1960s radical activist

Erotic politicians, that's what we are. We're interested in everything about revolt, disorder, and all activity that appears to have no meaning.
    Jim Morrison

[On "big business"]: They're willing to exploit John Doe and let America become a third-world country economically if it benefits them.

John Cougar Mellencamp

You can't be a politician with a guitar.

John Doe, X

[On Devo's commitment to spreading their philosophy of de-evolution]: We weren't doing it to have a good time or for fun, because those concepts are irrelevant to the bigger picture.

Mark Mothersbaugh

Pop music is usually so pretentious when it tries to be political.

Paul Simon

[Explaining the song, "The Children's Crusade"]: . . . History is, in part, a series of madmen deluding people into parting with their children for loathsome and tragic schemes.

Sting

[Political ruminations on Watergate, circa 1977]: Have you met Nixon? Is he happy? I saw him on TV last year and he looked so unhappy!

Michael Jackson

The American kids that disrupted their colleges and left them in a shambles, there wasn't an original thinker amongst the whole roll call. That's why in the end nothing came of it.

Anonmyous

[On how the media obsession with character issues killed his desire to seek public office]: If they had fun with Bill Clinton, what would they do with me?   **Stephen Stills**

We have too many people; we have to use birth control.   **Sting**

I don't know fuck about the U.N. I'd rather sing about rock 'n' roll and chicks.   **Tom Petty**

Even in the Reagan era, we could be uplifted by a song like Talking Heads' "Life During Wartime" or The Clash's "Rock the Casbah" or Prince's "Let's Go Crazy." Songs like those really helped to point a way out. I know that's what got me through the Eighties.   **Vernon Reid**, Living Colour

The only thing that could possibly save British politics would be Margaret Thatcher's assassin.   **Morrissey**

My father was a captain in the army; I guess I have a kinda war ting in me, but is better to die fighting for yar freedom than to be a prisoner all the days of yar life.   **Bob Marley**

PRETENSIONS

All my concerts had no sounds in them; they were completely silent. People had to make their own music in their minds. **Yoko Ono**

Pretentiousness is interesting; your ambition has to oustrip your ability at some point. **Anonymous**

The way I see it, rock 'n' roll is folk music. **Robert Plant**

[Justifying an aborted show in Philadelphia]: Performing there was like having an epileptic seizure in a subway. I felt nothing; so rather than fake an orgasm, I decided to get dressed and leave. **Perry Farrell**

A good piece of work shows you have taken a victorious position in the struggle with falsehoods. **Wynton Marsalis**

I have the devil in me! If I didn't, I'd be a Christian.

Jerry Lee Lewis

I like leaping around onstage, as long as it's done with class.
Ritchie Blackmore, Deep Purple

The MC5 is totally committed to the revolution. With our music and our economic genius, we plunder the suspecting straight world for money and the means to carry out our program—and revolutionize its children at the same time.
John Sinclair, manager, MC5

Rock 'n' roll is quite fun and everything, but I'm only using it as a medium.
David Bowie

I try not to repeat myself. It's the hardest thing in the world to do—there are only so many notes one human being can master.
Prince

RACISM

... It's not odd that black people play rock and roll—what's really odd is that people think it's odd.
Vernon Reid, Living Colour

It's like the early days of rock 'n' roll. The authorities paid no attention as long as it was a black thing, but as soon as white kids began aping black styles, they came down hard. **Luther Campbell**, 2 Live Crew

You must realize music has no prejudice itself; it's the people who make the difference. And when entertainers get together, they don't think in terms of who's old, who's you, who's white, who's black. We think in terms of combining the talents, and making it good and enjoyable to each other.

B.B. King

It's hard to imagine someone being racist.... [Without black music] we wouldn't have any of the music that we love. We'd be all these tight-assed WASPs doing jigs. **Lou Reed**

White people should make rock 'n' roll ... that's white music. They can't really make black music. **Billy Idol**

The media usually looks for one person—spokesperson—to be representative of black people. **Vanessa Williams**

I have never considered it a disadvantage to be a black woman. I never wanted to be anything else. We have brains. We are beautiful. We can do anything we set our minds to. **Diana Ross**

I've been "not black enough." When I became the first black Miss America, there was feedback that I wasn't representative of black America because I

didn't have true African-American features—my eyes are green, I have lighter skin.
Vanessa Williams

Rap is teaching white kids what it means to be black, and that causes a problem for the infrastructure.
Chuck D, Public Enemy

You can overcome any obstacle in this country. It may be a little harder for you than someone else. Like when Jackie Robinson got into baseball, he couldn't just be an average second baseman 'cause there were plenty of them around. He had to be better than what was already there.
Ray Charles

Irish-Americans are no more Irish than black Americans are Africans.
Bob Geldof

[On the recoring of his 1986 smash hit *Graceland*, partly recorded in South Africa]: I never said there were not strong political implications to what I did. I just said the music was not overtly political. But the implications of the music certainly are. And I still think it's the most powerful form of politics, more powerful than saying it right on the money, in which case you're usually preaching to the converted. People get attracted to the music, and once they hear what's going on within it, they say "What? They're doing that to these people?"
Paul Simon

REALITY

No matter how loud the guitar is and how much you jump around and sweat and get angst-ridden, eventually you have to go home, be polite, and kiss your mother on the cheek. **John Wilbur**, Superchunk

The dreams have been cashed in for reality and reality is so much sweeter than the dream. **Phillip Michael Thomas**

We tend to view classical music as this venerable and sacred thing. A guy like Mozart was simply a pop star of his day. Had he been around, he would have probably been in The Beatles on keyboard. **Paul McCartney**

[The recollection of a groupie and her friend Mary who, after a great deal of effort, succeeded in bedding Mick Jagger]: We were really disappointed. He was only so-so. He tried to come on like Mick Jagger, but he's no Mick Jagger. **Kathy**

A typical day in the life of a heavy-metal musician consists of a round of golf and an AA meeting. **Billy Joel**

It's easy to make disgusting, unlistenable records that are just plain weird, but that's what we do on a good day.   **David Was**, producer

An aspirin can cure a headache for an hour or two, but if the pain's really deep, nothing short of brain surgery is going to make it go away.

Ray Charles

[On being compared to immortal songwriters of the past]: It could be momentarily flattering. But then you realize that some people don't like Cole Porter.

Elvis Costello

For me it was like I was an old car and I was being taken out for a ride at one hundred mph; and I kind of liked it, because I was really getting rid of a lot of rust.   **Norman Mailer**, on attending a Ramones concert

There are moods I'm in when I can't stand to listen to some of my own music.   **Joni Mitchell**

Detroit turned out to be heaven, but it also turned out to be hell.

Marvin Gaye

Making a comeback is one of the most difficult things to do with dignity.

Greg Lake, Emerson, Lake, and Palmer

I don't think anybody steals anything; all of us borrow.   **B.B. King**

They keep 'em as clean as they possibly could, but prisons are to punish people, so they don't exactly have room service, you know.

Ozzy Osbourne

I'm older now. I see the world through different eyes. I still believe in love, peace, and understanding. As Elvis Costello said, "And what's so funny about love, peace, and understanding?"

John Lennon [said three days before his death]

Get plenty article that is pure foolishness. You have a guy come talk to you for a whole week, and him go an' write something for please the Devil.

Bob Marley

You don't shoulder any responsibility when you pick up a guitar or sing a song, because it's not a position of responsibility. **Keith Richards**

I'm not really a good enough singer to really enjoy it, but I am getting into it a little bit. I enjoy playing the guitar more than I enjoy singing, and I can't play the guitar, either. But I know that if I keep on playing the guitar, I can get better, where I can't improve much as a singer. **Mick Jagger**

Who isn't fascinated by evil? **Marvin Gaye**

When you walk into a performance situation or a record-company office, people really like you, they pay a lot of attention to you. But then, your normal life is the same as anybody's—just as lonely. You can't get anyone on the phone, and you can't get a date. **Ricki Lee Jones**

[On his biggest megahit, "Just the Way You Are"]: ... We weren't even serious about that song. Everybody was down on it and thought it was too goofy and sappy. Liberty [De Vito, the drummer] didn't even want to play on it. "I'm not Tito Puente!" he said. "I won't play that oily cocktail lounge cha-cha/samba crap!"   **Billy Joel**

Music can't change the world.   **Bob Geldof**

If you're in this business for more than five years, you become a boring old fart.   **Brian Travers**

REBELLION

I'm a rebel, a brat. That's the way rock musicians are.   **Bryan Adams**

The youth rebellion is a worldwide phenomenon that has not been seen before in history. I do not believe they will calm down and be ad execs at thirty as the Establishment would like us to believe.

William S. Burroughs, author

If you are going to kick authority in the teeth, you might as well use two feet.
Keith Richards

That's the problem that rock 'n' roll poses—to be or not to be a rebel. That's what it says and always has said. **David Bowie**

If you're writing songs, there are two things that you just don't write about: politics and religion. We write about both. **Bono**

There is always gonna be an element that doesn't like rock 'n' roll. But as long as I keep it clean and within FCC guidelines, I say, "Fuck 'em."
Charlie Kendall, WNEW-FM

I enjoy getting people angry and getting underneath their skin, especially people who don't think. **Jello Biafra**, The Dead Kennedys

Why the fuck hasn't there been a female Jimi Hendrix, a female guitar great? Because no one ever put in the effort and stuck to it. I thought, "I'm going to get up there and fucking do it myself." **Lita Ford**

I personally do not consider Pepsi-Cola or Old Style Beer or the Health and Tennis Corporation to be the enemy. This is the age of adult rock stars. You can't be James Dean all of your life. **Glenn Frey**, The Eagles

What do bored kids do when they don't play rock 'n' roll? They torture cats, they do burglaries. **Kim Thayil**, Soundgarden

The reason kids like rock 'n' roll is because their parents don't.

Mitch Miller

Obviously, being in a rock band makes you more adolescent than if you worked in an IBM company and really had to worry about your future. I don't worry about the future. I'm living out my adolescent dreams perpetually. My mother has always been unhappy with what I do. She would much rather I do something nicer, like be a bricklayer.   **Mick Jagger**

I'm into revolution and radicalism and changing the whole world structure.

Kathleen Hanna, Bikini Kill

I am interested in anything about revolt, disorder, chaos, especially activity that seems to have no meaning.   **Jim Morrison**

Say it loud, I'm black and I'm proud.   **James Brown**

As far as I'm concerned, fuck Seattle!

Billy Corgan, Smashing Pumpkins

I don't give a fuck about rock 'n' roll.   **Sting**

RECOVERY

The fun thing about being sober is meeting all the friends I've had for years, especially the ones I've never met.
                                                                    Alice Cooper

There are two things I respect in life. One is anyone who can stay in this business longer than two albums, and two is anyone who can beat their addiction, no matter what it is. Drugs, food, gambling—everyone has an addiction.
                                                    Nikki Sixx, Mötley Crüe

Take the drugs away and there's more time for sex and rock 'n' roll.
                        Steven Tyler, Aerosmith, after four rehab sessions

[About seeking help for his alcoholism]: I hope people will say, "God, if he can go for help, so can I."
                                                                    Ringo Starr

This is the highest I've ever been in my entire, entire life. I feel so good. I just got back from the gym, and Steven Tyler and Joe Perry ... were there working out. And you're gonna tell us we ain't bad boys? This feeling kicks ass.
                                                                    Nikki Sixx

I used to worry that if you took away all my neuroses, where would I be and what would I have? But after giving up drugs and drink and going through therapy, I find I didn't lose my feelings. If anything, I feel more poetic and exposed. **Marianne Faithfull**

[Happy Mondays leader on his entering rehab for his addiction to heroin]: I thought, "This time I'm doing it for moi." **Shaun Ryder**

Sex is so much better! It's amazing! My wife is thrilled! She's like, "Oh, my God! This is the shit, man!" **Tommy Lee**, Mötley Crüe

RELATIONSHIPS

My guitar is the only thing in my life that hasn't fucked me over.
Dave Mustaine, Megadeth

[On his legendarily troubled and abusive marriage to Tina Turner]: If I had it to do all over again, I wouldn't do anything any different. Except maybe for all the girlfriends. **Ike Turner**

I'm leaving the group. I want a divorce. **John Lennon**

When you're in a relationship, you're always surrounded by a ring of circumstances—joined together by a wedding ring, or in a boxing ring.

Bob Seger

Ninety-nine percent of the male population of the Western world—and beyond—would give a limb to live the life of Jagger, to *be* Mick Jagger. And he's not happy being Mick Jagger. To me, that's unacceptable. I've got to make him happy! To me, I've failed if I can't eventually get my mate to feel good about himself—even though he's very autocratic and he can be a real asshole. But who can't be an asshole at times? **Keith Richards**

I introduced Yoko to John Lennon. Lennon used to come into the gallery quite often—he was a pal.... Yoko was one of the artists I exhibited. That kind of thing. I thought John would like her, so I invited him to one of her openings and got them together. I don't think he liked any of her stuff, but he bought one anyway. **John Dunbar**, gallery owner

[On why she divorced James Taylor]: Basically, he just wasn't willing to dress up like Louis IV before we went to bed every night. I really demand that of a partner. **Carly Simon**

Everybody gives off a certain musical note. I think I'm F-sharp. The thing is you can go around and you meet somebody who's in F-sharp, you're in harmony, see. But if you meet somebody who's in F-unng, it's a discord: you don't get on. **Donovan**

If you escape from people too often, you wind up escaping from yourself.

Marvin Gaye

Just because you're married doesn't mean you're in love.   **Rick James**

I wouldn't have any desire to be a traditional wife, and frankly, I don't know what man would want to put up with me.   **Linda Ronstadt**

My husband is German. Last night I dressed up as Poland and he invaded me.   **Bette Midler**

Sooner or later, we all sleep alone. . . .   **Bob Seger**

People often ask me what I look for in women. I look for ME in women!

Gene Simmons

At a certain point, a man wants to own you, and no man will ever own me.

Grace Jones

Mick [Jagger] and I are incredibly diverse people. . . . While a certain part of our personalities is incredibly close, there's an awful lot which is very, very different. I'm his friend and he knows it. It's just, like, "I love you, darling, but I can't live with you."   **Keith Richards**

[On the recording of her and former husband Richard Thompson's classic album *Shoot Out the Lights*]: I think we both were miserable and didn't quite know how to get it out—I think that's why the album is so good. We couldn't talk to each other, so we just did it on the record.

Linda Thompson

I'm too busy for dating and girls right now. I'd like to try, maybe. What do you think? Think I should, yeah? Well, I'll think about that.

Michael Jackson

[On her friendship with fellow musicians Tom Waits and Chuck E. Weiss]: It seems sometimes like we're really romantics who got stuck in the wrong time zone.   **Ricki Lee Jones**

[On an early date with sex-bomb Britt Eckland]: I took her to an all-night laundry; we watched her bra go 'round in the machine.   **Rod Stewart**

[On husband Eddie Van Halen]: I can't say that we're really great friends— we don't have a helluva lot in common—but we'll always be connected like brother and sister. That helps when the romance comes and goes.

Valerie Bertinelli, actress

RELIGION & SPIRITUALITY

Christianity will go. It will vanish and shrink. . . . We're more popular than Jesus now. I don't know which will go first—rock 'n' roll or Christianity.

John Lennon

If you want to live with the Lord, you can't rock 'n' roll it, too. God don't like it.

Little Richard

Most of my songs are about Jesus. Most of my songs are about the idea that there is salvation, and that there is a Savior. But I won't mention his name in a song just to get a cheap play.

Pete Townshend

[Legendary mystic recounts the advice he gave the young Bob Marley]: If a mon lives upright, ya cyan speak and make lightning; ya cyan speak and it is done; and you will command it will stand fast, but ya have to live a clean life! People have to try an' live up. I've seen a lot of little miracles in the night. I'm a fisherman; I fish for a long while and in the night I see the sky move! Sometime ya cyan see for yourself—ya find t'ings jus' done in front of yuh, and it looks like miracles.

Countryman

My mother knew her polio was not a curse, but a test that God gave her to triumph over. And she instilled in me a love of Him that I will always have.
Michael Jackson

When one finds himself, one finds God. You find God and you find yourself.
Prince

The perfect relationship is the one between Jesus and heavenly Father.
Marvin Gaye

Pain is another word for fear. True believers have no fear.
Marvin Gaye

The Devil is a very generous mon—he'll give you everything for your soul!
Bob Marley

If God wants me to become a woman, then a woman I will become.
Mick Jagger

There is nothing written in the Bible, Old or New Testament, that says, "If you believe in Me, you ain't going to have no troubles."
Ray Charles

RIVALRIES

Comparing Madonna with Marilyn Monroe is like comparing Raquel Welch with the back of a bus.   **Boy George**

Boy George makes me sick.   **Madonna**

[About the Sex Pistols singer Johnny Rotten]: John's just jealous because I'm the brains of the group. I've written all the songs, even from the beginning when I wasn't in the group. They were so useless, they had to come to me because they couldn't think of anything by themselves.   **Sid Vicious**

I don't like people like Rod Stewart and Elton John, and I don't like the way they carry on. I get very upset at being identified with that kind of person.
Mick Jagger, 1978

I think Townshend's always wanted to be me.   **Roger Daltry**, 1975

. . . I'll wear anything as long as it hasn't been on George Michael's back.
Boy George

I gave up rock 'n' roll for the rock of ages! I used to be a glaring homosexual until God changed me!

Little Richard

[On Vanity, leader of the Prince-formed girl-group Vanity 6]: ... Her I.Q. is equivalent to her new bra size ... must be 32 now. I have nothing positive to say about her. She never taught me anything about film or music or anything worth having a conversation about.　　　　　**Appollonia**

The Smiths are more important than The Police! We're more important than they ever were, or ever will be.　　　　　**Johnny Marr**, 1984

THE ROAD

If anybody asks you what kind of music you play, tell him "pop." Don't tell him "rock 'n' roll," or they won't even let you in the hotel.

Buddy Holly

Being on tour sends me crazy. I drink too much and out comes the John McEnroe in me.　　　　　**Chrissie Hynde**

The road isn't a religion. It's part of how I make my income. That itch to hit the road is gone. I like my life now. I used to be afraid of being in my forties. Now I find out my forties are pretty good. Of course, I'm rich and

I'm married to Christie Brinkley. And that will tend to skew one's view of things.   **Billy Joel**, December 1993 (pre-divorce)

I always start out the first week I'm on tour running every day. I try to eat right. Then there's always a night when I didn't get enough sleep so I don't run; and I'm afraid of eating so I do some cocaine; and I was depressed that night so I take an upper; and then that's the end of it. Then it's uppers and coke for the rest of the tour.   **Linda Ronstadt**

We were barred from so many hotels, the entire Holiday Inn chain, that we had to check in as Fleetwood Mac lots of times.

                                    Ronnie Wood, on The Faces

Being on the road hasn't tarnished our viewpoints toward women. If anything, it's made us better in bed.   **Dave Mustaine**, Megadeth

James [Christian] was walking onstage and calling the city by the wrong name. He said, "Hello, Cleveland," in Columbus. The audience's faces fell. Then a lot of people went to the airport to book flights to Columbus.

                                    Greg Giuffria, House of Lords

I don't care if we have to go out and open Fotomats. We've been off the road for four months, and I miss it. I get so excited just rehearsing with this band. And you can kill yourself easier at home than you can out there.

                                    Chris Robinson, Black Crowes

I'd been out with Dylan's Rolling Thunder Revue, which was an amazing experience, studying mysticism and ego malfunction like you wouldn't believe. Everybody took all their vices to the nth degree and came out of it born again or into AA. **Joni Mitchell**

There aren't as many groupies as there used to be.

K.K. Downing, Judas Priest

There isn't a town in the world I haven't run amok in. **Joe Strummer**

[About the Sex Pistols]: It's a real feeling of déjà vu. They puked at the London airport; we pissed in the filling station. **Keith Richards**

ROCK 'N' ROLL

It will be gone by June. *Variety*, 1955

The story has got pretty crowded as to who was the Father of Rock 'n' Roll. I haven't done much in life except that. And I'd like to get credit for it.

Bill Haley (of The Comets)

Rock 'n' roll is trying to convince girls to pay money to be near you.
Richard Hell, The Voidoids

There'll always be some arrogant little brat who wants to make music with a guitar. Rock 'n' roll will never die.   **Dave Edmunds**

Rock is a corruption of rhythm and blues, which was a dilution of the blues, so that today's mass-marketed noise is a vulgarization of a vulgarization.
Benny Green, *This Is Jazz*, 1960

Rock 'n' roll is a bit like Las Vegas; guys dressed up in their sisters' clothes pretending to be rebellious and angry, but not really angry about anything.
Sting

Rock 'n' roll actually wasn't invented by anybody, and it's not just black and white either. It's Mexican and Appalachian and Gaelic and everything that's come floating down the river.   **T-Bone Burnett**

Rock 'n' roll is an asylum for emotional imbeciles.   **Richard Neville**

Poison put to sound.   **Pablo Casals**, classical musician (cellist)

Rock 'n' roll was getting up there, stepping out, and creating the greatest possible imperfection.   **Malcolm McLaren**

The end of World War II and the way the world changed in the wake of those cataclysms is what caused rock 'n' roll—not the other way around.

Daryl Hall, Hall & Oates

At what point did rhythm and blues start becoming rock 'n' roll? When the white kids started to dance to it.

Ruth Brown, rhythm and blues singer

Rock 'n' roll is so great that everyone in the world should think it's the greatest thing that's happening. If they don't, they're turds.

Lux Interior, The Cramps

Rock 'n' roll is a communicable disease.

The New York Times, 1956

Rock 'n' roll is beautiful and it's ugly simultaneously. I mean, it's rock 'n' roll that brings people together in the mud in Woodstock. It's rock 'n' roll that starts black riots in Rochester and has cops beating people on the head for ten hours later. It's rock 'n' roll, you know. There's so many good things, and so many bad things. It's so unpredictable.

Howard Stern, radio personality

It's not music, it's a disease.

Mitch Miller

I think Adolph Hitler discovered rock 'n' roll. I mean, he was the guy who started with the kids in the street. He went straight past the parents. . . .

Pete Townshend

It will be the end of us.   **Bridget O'Donnell**, writer

Rock 'n' roll can mean many things, but it must not stay in the same place.
Bono

Rock 'n' roll deals with the acting out of your emotional, conscience-oriented, and sexual feelings in front of someone. . . . And feelings expressed that directly can prove offensive to some people.   **Daryl Hall**

By the eighties, a lot of radio stations had started playing Sixties' music. They called it "classic rock," because they knew we'd be upset if they came right out and called it what it is, namely "middle-aged person nostalgia music."
Dave Barry, humorist

Rock 'n' roll is ridiculous. It's absurd. In the past, U2 was trying to duck that. Now we're wrapping our arms around it and giving it a great big kiss. It's like I say onstage, "Some of this bullshit is pretty cool."   **Bono**

Though rock 'n' roll is over thirty years old, no one has really tried to make it grow up.   **Keith Richards**

Rock 'n' roll all goes back to R and B, but to me it's not very relevant. Kraftwerk is much more relevant.   **Nick Rhodes**, Duran Duran

Rock and roll has become respectable. What a bummer.   **Ray Davies**

No crybabies allowed in rock and roll!

attributed to **Ted Nugent** by Bob Seger

The main purpose of rock 'n' roll is celebration of the self. And the only evil in rock 'n' roll is deliberately directed mindlessness—which is a good definition for evil in general.　　　　**Daryl Hall**, Hall & Oates

The bigger you get, the less you have to work—which is never a good thing for a musician. . . . The truth is, I'm more interested in the roll than I am in the rock.　　　　**Keith Richards**

Rock 'n' roll music is here to stay.　　　　**Alan Freed**

SELF-IMAGE

I wish people would understand that I always thought I was bad. I wouldn't have got into the business if I didn't think I was bad.　　**Prince**

I've always been a great fan of diversification, eh? At one period I had the whole lot going. I was a Buddhist mime songwriter and part-time sax player. . . .
David Bowie

My defenses were so great. The cocky rock 'n' roll hero who knows all the answers was actually a terrified guy who didn't know how to cry. Simple.

John Lennon

I have an old spirit.

Anita Baker

Sometimes when I see my face taking up a whole page of a magazine, I hate that guy.

Eddie Vedder

I'm actually quite a decent chap, and the rest of the group are wankers.

Jools Holland, Squeeze

I'm an instant star; just add water and stir.

David Bowie

I've just had the handles taken off my back. I used to be a shopping cart at Von's, I was pushed around so much.

Gregg Giuffria, House of Lords

I am not a saint. I am a noise.

Joan Baez

I look at what's there. What's there is legs and hair.

Tina Turner

I live pretty much of a normal life and do all the things other kids do. I don't know why everyone thinks I'm so much different.

Michael Jackson

I was considering doing a song with Billy Idol. That would have been good because we're both white and plastic and blond.

Madonna

I'm a black sheep; in fact, I'm a black sheep of black sheep—I understand my father was a black sheep, too.   **Jerry Garcia**

You think I'm an asshole now, you should have seen me when I was drunk.
                                                      John Cougar Mellencamp

I don't want to become Tracy Chapman or Sinéad O'Connor. All my life, growing up in the suburbs, I've been completely shut out, and I've always been the weirdo. And the last thing I want is for people to all of a sudden appreciate what I do. . . . It's not romantic, the whole record-company-magazine-interview thing. I like to be with my girlfriend. I like to be in bed and rent movies. That's life.   **Anonymous**

I can't hardly sing, you know what I mean? I'm no Tom Jones, and I couldn't give a fuck.   **Mick Jagger**

There are three layers to me. The first is alert, amiable, and at ease with the world. Then there is the sad, small boy. In all, there is this instinctive and at times aggressive character. I fluctuate between the three, but the stranger, the third layer only comes out in the music.   **Peter Gabriel**

I call myself a hopeful cynic.   **Tracy Chapman**

SEX

I've been known to forget to un-handcuff a few girls.

Stiv Bators, Dead Boys

In one way, what genuinely turned me on was the music. There's a great relationship between the music and the body, and the musician who makes you feel so good, you quite often sleep with him out of gratitude. . . . I suppose in a way it's a kind of "Thank you, what can I do for you?"

Jenny Fabian, author of *Groupie*

Do I enjoy having sex? Yes, I'd be crazy not to. I was deprived in high school, and I'm gonna make up for it now.   **Bret Michaels**, Poison

If sex is such a natural phenomenon, how come there are so many books on "how to"?   **Bette Midler**

Beyond sex is God.   **Marvin Gaye**

If I was a girl, I'd rather fuck a rock star than a plumber.

Gene Simmons

Rock 'n' roll since its inception has always been more sexually subversive than politically subversive.   **Stephen Mallinder**, Cabaret Voltaire

Michael's [bandmate Lardia] like the perfectionist workaholic orgy man. . . . He's got more women than the fuckin' toilet seat of the YWCA.

Jack Russell, Great White

I've gone through a whoring stage. That's fine, it's good to learn what it's like to be a whore.   **Perry Farrell**

Passions are dangerous. They cause you to lust after other men's wives.

Marvin Gaye

Everybody expects us to walk around with socks on our dicks.

Anthony Kiedis, Red Hot Chili Peppers

A long time ago, I used to get drunk and hang out a lot around mental institutions; because the girls there are all loose and they are . . . fun, you know?   **Joey Ramone**

[On Mick Jagger]: When a performer can actually turn on both men and women, that's quite sophisticated. That's not just wiggling your ass.

Phil May

SEXISM

Rock 'n' roll is for men. Real rock 'n' roll is a man's job. I want to see a man up there. I want to see a man's muscles, a man's veins. I don't want to see no chick's tit banging against a bass.　　　　**Patti Smith**

Even though I was a big seller, they only cared about males.

Lesley Gore

A lot of chicks come up to me and ask me—in fact, it used to piss me off, I must say—"How does it feel being a chick playing guitar?" The minute that I would hear that remark, I would just want to hit them.

Alice Stewart

After we sold three or four million albums, we thought we wouldn't be treated like an all-girl band anymore, but as a rock 'n' roll band. That never really worked.　　　　**Belinda Carlisle**

There's really no reason to have women on tour, unless they've got a job to do. The only other reason is to screw. Otherwise, they get bored. They just sit around and moan.　　　　**Mick Jagger**

You have to be twice as smart, twice as tough, and twice as good as the men just to get to the bottom of the rank where you can eat and pay your rent.

Anonymous

Someone said, "Wear this," and we'd go "Oh, okay." The Runaways were out there just for the boys.

Lita Ford

Girl-type screams are silly. When you get a guy that screams—an appreciative-type yell—encouragement, that can kind of turn you on when you're performing.

Rod Stewart

STORIES

One night John [Lennon] and I were sitting in the [Tokyo] living room. . . . He started playing "Jealous Guy." Now, I can't tell you how big this living room was. All of a sudden, the elevator doors opened and a Japanese couple walked in. They were obviously dressed for dinner. They walked around and looked out at the view of Tokyo, and then sat down. John kept playing. They lit cigarettes and talked. I suddenly realized that they thought they were in the lounge of the restaurant. They took a wrong turn, came into a huge, very dark room, where there was a lounge musician playing guitar and singing in a foreign language, and there was one other guest, waiting. They had a cigarette or two, and I guess it was because no waiter had arrived to take their order that they finally looked at John, exchanged some words, and got up and left, obviously displeased. That was John Lennon's last public performance.

Elliot Mintz, journalist and publicist

... He'd [Michael Jackson] say, "Paul, I need some advice." I'd give him that advice and say, "Look, get good financial people, people you can trust." I took him under my wing, and we'd always be in little corridors, discussing this stuff. I thought it was just fine, but he used to tell this little joke: he'd say, [mimicking Jackson's meek tone] "I'm gonna buy your publishing, ya know." I'd go, "Ha! Good one, kid!" Then one day I get phoned up and they said, "He's just bought your stuff." I thought, "Oh, you are kidding."

Paul McCartney

To succeed [as a groupie], you had to have an attention-getter, like the Plaster-Casters, who were a couple of middle-class girls from the Chicago area: "Excuse me, we're making this collection of erect penises, we've already got Jefferson Airplane, The Animals, and Led Zeppelin—we would like to add yours to the collection. What? You'd like to see some of the others—why, of course, we'll bring them up to your room—they're all autographed."

Jenny Fabian, author of *Groupie*

I remember the guys in the Air Force saying, "Don't step on my blue suede shoes." I thought it was a good line and told Carl (Perkins) he should put it into a song. But he wrote it all. It's his song. **Johnny Cash**

[About "Maggie May," the song that made him a star]: I was nearly persuaded to take that off the album. A mate I was knocking about with at the time said he didn't think it had anything melodic to offer. I sort of agreed with him, but it was too late because we didn't have any more tracks. . . . When it came out on a single, it was a B-side; "Reason to Believe" was the A-side. And it was a disc jockey in Cleveland, I believe, that turned it over. Otherwise, I wouldn't be here today. I'd still be digging graves in the cemetery.

Rod Stewart

I'd do these disappearing acts. I'd pass through some seedy town with a pinball arcade, fall in with people who worked on the machines, people staying alive shoplifting, whatever. They don't know who you are: "Why are you driving that white Mercedes? Oh, you're driving it for somebody else." You know, make up some name and hang out. Great experiences, almost like *The Prince and the Pauper*.   **Joni Mitchell**

I was twenty-one years old, and I came out to L.A. in a pickup truck with everything I owned in the back. I told everyone I was going to be a rock star. Two years later, I was in a number one band. If it can happen to me, it can happen to anyone.   **Gina Shock**, The Go-Gos

We punched a clock, literally punched a clock, nine o'clock in the morning. That was the procedure at Motown. Berry Gordy had worked at Ford, so he ran Motown like a factory.   **Lamont Dozier**

When it ended [the screening of their film on The Rolling Stones infamous Altamont concert, *Gimme Shelter*], [producer Joseph E.] Levine turned to his assistant and said, "Who is Mick Jagger anyway?" His assistant replied that he was a great rock 'n' roll star. "Well," said Joe Levine, "he's no Sammy Davis," and walked out. **David and Albert Maysles**

I can recall going back into his [bluesman Freddie King] dressing room, and he would show me his gun and his knife, and then we would finish off a bottle of gin before he went on. The man was a hurricane—he was unbelievable—and there would always be a couple of spent women lying around.

Eric Clapton

Down in D.C., they were talking about the go-go; but I had them kids out in the streets while they were still babies, doing the popcorn with the Original Disco Man. Funk I invented back in the fifties. The rap thing I had down on my "Brother Rapp (Part I)," and you can check that.... Michael Jackson, he used to watch me from the wings and got his moonwalk from my camelwalk—he'll tell you that if you ask. Same way, I was slippin' and slidin' before Prince was out of his crib; that's why Alan Leeds, who used to work for my organization, is on his management team, tipping and hipping him. I ain't jealous, I'm zealous. I ain't teased, I'm pleased. Who's gonna do James Brown better'n James Brown? **James Brown**

He took my music. But he gave me my name.

Muddy Waters, on Mick Jagger

There's a man in West Memphis, has a recording studio there. He recorded me once ... but he ain't never gonna do it again. He gave my song to someone else, and put it out on record, and says that he's written it. So he got money for the song. That motherfucker! I went there to his house in West Memphis and hid in the grass outside his house with a pistol. But when I was gonna shoot him, his wife came home. I was mad. I would have shot him.

John "Red" Williams, songwriter

[About recording *East Side Story* with Elvis Costello as producer]: One morning Elvis called and said that John Lennon had been killed the night before, and that we weren't going to go out to the studio that day. Then he called back and said, "No, let's just go in, get some drink, and play." We didn't record anything; we were just playing the blues."

Chris Difford

TITLES

I think the first song I ever wrote . . . was called "Can't Help Thinking About Me." That's an illuminating little piece, isn't it?

David Bowie

[Song title]: "My Head Hurts, My Feet Stink, and I Don't Love Jesus."

Jimmy Buffett

[Song title]: "God is a Real-Estate Developer."

Michelle Shocked

[On the title of his 1986 album *So*]: I liked the shape, and the fact that it didn't have too much meaning. **Peter Gabriel**

TRUTH IN ADVERTISING?

Sometimes I'm not sure what a lot of our songs are about.

Jim Kerr, Simple Minds

I can't do anything else. **Jerry Garcia**

There's no message to heavy metal. . . . It's about being rich and famous and getting laid.

Penelope Spheeris, director of a documentary on the music

Let's face it, I'm a showoff. **Peter Frampton**

We were so awkward, musically speaking, when we got together as a band. We couldn't really play our instruments or anything. But that didn't stop us from playing them. **Bono**

Cosmetics is a boon to every woman, but a girl's best friend is still a near-sighted man.

Yoko Ono

I'm the proverbial good time that was had by all.

Cher

[On why The Moody Blues changed from the blues to the classical-influenced progressive rock they ultimately became known for]: It was really because at that point we'd gone as far as we could go singing about people's problems in the Deep South of America without knowing anything about it. . . .

Justin Hayward

We don't always know what we're doing. We often just get excited, put something down, and say, "Oh, neat."

Tina Weymouth, Talking Heads

People should realize, we are just jerks like them.

Bono

Listening to me has ruined a lot of other singers. A lot of singers who have tried to sound like me, they sound like they're going through so much pain.

Rod Stewart

I'm not really a good singer. But most people aren't, either.

Robyn Hitchcock

I think it's also fair to say that this band says some of the stupidest things amongst themselves that I've ever heard anybody say.

Spencer Sercombe, Shark Island

It's an admission of humanity. You can't just scream and holler all your life. You have to step back a minute, look at yourself, and say, "Yeah, I am fucked." And try to change it. **Bob Mould**, Hüsker Dü, Sugar

People think The Beatles know what's going on. We don't. We're just doing it. **John Lennon**

I never know how much of what I say is true. **Bette Midler**

I'm barely prolific and incredibly lazy. **Tom Petty**

We're playing at our own level of ability. **Dee Dee Ramone**

Steve can go off and be Peter Frampton; Sid can go off and kill himself and nobody will care; Paul can go back to being an electrician; and Malcolm will always be a Wally.
Johnny Rotten (John Lydon), on the disintegration of the Sex Pistols

That's what we're all about; taking advantage of people.
Lars Ulrich, Metallica

There is no live set. I just make it up as I go along.
Jonathan Richman, The Modern Lovers

WE ARE THE WORLD

[Instructions to the superstars with whom he recorded, "We Are the World"]: Check your egos at the door.

Quincy Jones

Make your success work to help others achieve their measures of success, and hope they, in turn, will do likewise. This is the kind of chain reaction that is music to my ears.

Berry Gordy

I know that in going to Central America, I was really moved to want to do something—to talk about whether we really believe in freedom and justice for all or if it isn't just freedom and justice for us, while we do the most unspeakable things to other cultures.... And there's a certain comfort, a security that I have, talking about something that I feel this strongly about. And whether or not an album succeeds wildly or not, that's intact.

Jackson Browne

It seems funny and peculiar that, after my [Farm-Aid] shows and Willie's [Nelson] shows, people come up to us for advice. It is because they have got nobody to turn to.

John Cougar Mellencamp

It was nice to see music guys you thought were just always being so concerned. . . . Often you find that your musicians do more good than your bloody government does. Certainly on Live Aid they did.

Paul McCartney

I'm all for sociological lyrics. I just can't be bothered to write them.

Suggs, Madness

Live Aid makes us feel a bit more comfortable to slightly relieve the discomfort of a nation in famine. But really the only way we can make them much more comfortable is by enduring a much higher level of discomfort ourselves. And we're not willing to do that. I'm not willing to do that. And I think that is evil. **Pete Townshend**

What it comes down to for me is: will the technologies of communication and culture—and especially popular music, which is a vast and beloved enterprise—help us to understand one another better, or will they deceive us and keep us apart? While there's still time, we all have to answer for ourselves.

Roger Waters, Pink Floyd

WRITING

A song is a message, a song is a letter, nothing more, nothing less.
Pete Townshend

I don't know what real childbirth is like, but writing songs seems as close as I'm going to come.
Billy Joel

I've written my best things when I'm upset. What's the point of sitting down and notating your happiness?
Madonna

I used to pretend that Tchaikovsky could compose through me, and it worked.
Anonymous

I don't deserve the Songwriters Hall of Fame Award. But fifteen years ago, I had a brain operation and I didn't deserve that, either. So I'll keep it.
Quincy Jones

I know some lines are bad when I write them. That's sort of perverted, isn't it?
Jane Siberry

When you write a song that sounds really good . . . you think, surely it must be someone else's. **Pete Shelley**, The Buzzcocks

[On the early, early, early days of U2]: . . . We would try to play other people's songs, but we just couldn't play them. We played them so badly, we decided to write our own songs. **Bono**

If you're gonna write songs, you've gotta have a life. It's as simple as that. Words and language are the most important things we have.

Don Henley

I refuse to slap some stupid words on the stupid paper just so we have a stupid song finished. **Suzanne Vega**

[That's] a familiar theme for me: looking into the darkness and seeing if there's a possibility for triumph. **Peter Gabriel**

It's important to me to make sure the average person can understand what I'm trying to say. Songwriting at its best is very rarely poetry; it's usually narrative and practically journalism. It's a form of literature, but one you can consume while you're driving your car.

Steve Earle, songwriter, country-rock musician

I realized right away I could write songs, because I could have experiences without even having them. **Stevie Nicks**